Clipper Studies in the Theatre
Number Seven
ISSN 0748-237X

The Trial of Dr. Jekyll

An Adaptation of Robert Louis Stevenson's
"The Strange Case of Dr. Jekyll and Mr. Hyde"

a Play *in* Two Acts

by

William L. Slout

AN EMERITUS ENTERPRISE BOOK

Distributed by **The Borgo Press**
San Bernardino, California
1993

THE BORGO PRESS
Publishers Since 1975
Post Office Box 2845
San Bernardino, CA 92406
United States of America

* * * * * * *

Copyright © 1989, 1993 by William L. Slout

All production rights reserved.
No part of this book may be reproduced in any form without the expressed written consent of the publisher. Printed in the United States of America by Van Volumes, Ltd. Cover design by Highpoint Type & Graphics. For production rights, contact William L. Slout, 2995 Ladera Road, San Bernardino, California 92405.

Library of Congress Cataloging-in-Publication Data

Slout, William L. (William Lawrence)
  The trial of Dr. Jekyll : an adaptation of Robert Louis Stevenson's The strange case of Dr. Jekyll and Mr. Hyde : a play in two acts / by William L. Slout.
    p. cm. (Clipper studies in the theatre, ISSN 0748-237X ; no. 7)
  "An Emeritus Enterprise book."
  ISBN 0-8095-6252-9 (cloth). — ISBN 0-8095-6253-7 (pbk.)
    1. Physicians—England—London—Drama. 2. Supernatural—Drama. I. Stevenson, Robert Louis, 1850-1894. Strange case of Dr. Jekyll and Mr. Hyde. II. Title. III. Series.
PS3569.L698T75 1993   93-10112
812'.54—dc20   CIP

FIRST EDITION

*To
Doug Buckhout,
dear friend
and
consumate stage Jekyll*

THE TRIAL OF DR. JEKYLL was first produced by the University Theatre at California State University, San Bernardino, on February 5, 1993, under the direction of William L. Slout and with the following cast and technical staff:

Dr. Henry Jekyll	Doug Buckhout
Questioner	Luke Hunt
Mr. Richard Enfield	Tex Acosta
Mr. Edward Hyde	Doug Buckhout
Mr. John C. Utterson	Orville Mendoza
Dr. Westley Lanyon	Michael Prather
Poole	Patrick Weeks
Miss Louise Gillian	Jennifer Tafolla
Inspector Quirk	Alva Moring
Mrs. Mordant	Wendi Hastings
SCENIC and LIGHTING DESIGNER	Lee Lyons
COSTUME and MAKEUP DESIGNER	Margaret Perry
SOUND DESIGNER	Andy Cameron
STAGE MANAGER	Greg Renne
ASSISTANT STAGE MANAGER	Jennifer Salbino

Photographs by DAN MOSELEY

AUTHOR'S NOTES

I have had a continuing interest in Stevenson's story of this two-sided, tragic hero, Dr. Henry Jekyll. Since its first publication, "The Strange Case of Dr. Jekyll and Mr. Hyde" has been dramatized by every performance medium, always making the most of the melodramatic elements inherent within it by adding a variety of sensational plot and character devices. In adapting the story, my intention was to return to the true incidents of Stevenson's invention, to purify the myth of Jekyll and Hyde. Consequently, the events of "The Trial of Dr. Jekyll" are the very ones Stevenson originated. The difference lies in the manner of telling the story. I chose to dramatize Jekyll's inner turmoil by the use of an imaginary court room, wherein, while writing his last statement and confession, Jekyll attempts to determine the extent of his guilt by fantacizing himself on trial.

The use of this device allows the sequence of events to flow without encumbrance and with the use of only a small amount of scenic paraphernalia. The characters walk out of scenes and into the witness box, and the reverse, straightforwardly and with no apology. The Questioner, the element of conscience in Jekyll, is never in the forefront; rather, always in shadow, nearly obscure but for his persistent prodding. The characters being questioned, directionalize their answers full front, as if the audience were the prosecutor.

Lee Lyons' scene design for the original production at California Stage University, San Bernardino, served the play well. A false proscenium, with doors on either side, was constructed on the university's thrust stage. Directly behind this was a scrim curtain. Behind the scrim, there was a judge's bench flanked by jury boxes and occupied by mannequins who sat stoically in dim lighting throughout the performance. The witness box slid into place in front of the proscenium when the scrim rolled up to reveal the court room. Scenes were performed in areas on both sides of this.

I caution against all artificial elements that smack of sentimentality and melodramatic effect. The transformations from Jekyll to Hyde and Hyde to Jekyll require no artifice of costume and makeup. The actor is all. His changing countenance and decorum between the two characters, if ably done, will satisfy the imagination of the audience. The use of non-melodic sound is indicated, rather than the traditional scoring of highlights with music. When done with restraint, it can punctuate and enhance without interfering.

CAST OF CHARACTERS

Dr. Henry Jekyll: A forty-two year old London medical doctor and scientist, is highly respected by his peers as a man of good will and charitable pursuits. HE prides himself in this reputation and devotes HIS energies toward upholding it. As a party-loving bachelor, HIS social gatherings are looked forward to by HIS many friends of reputable position. However, there is another side of JEKYLL, a love of wanton revelry, to which HE increasingly succumbs but ardently conceals.

Questioner: An exact image of JEKYLL, and an element of JEKYLL'S moral self, HE is dogged in HIS quest for answers, at times impatient, yet able to find humor in HIS interrogations.

Mr. Richard Enfield: A bachelor, closing in on forty years of age, HE has an accountant's preciseness. HE is somewhat lacking in humor and fearful of offending. Although a kinsman of UTTERSON, HIS social activities are restricted by HIS slightly lower station.

Mr. Edward Hyde: JEKYLL'S other self is a twisted young man, the epitome of evil. This is apparent in the raspiness of HIS speech, the deformity of HIS physical nature, and the aura of his persona. HE is quick to anger, yet impish with diabolical humor.

Mr. John C. Utterson: In HIS early forties, HE is a prominent London solicitor, greatly respected, conservative in his views but amiable in manner.

Dr. Westley Lanyon: Of an age with UTTERSON and JEKYLL, and a college chum, HE is a prominent physician with strong views and a tendency toward excitability.

Poole: A man of medium age, HE is JEKYLL'S efficient and trusted house man of long standing.

Miss Louise Gillian: An unwed lady of thirty-some, SHE is the upstairs maid for a well-to-do family. HER life, cloistered by the nature of HER occupation, has been limited to the mundane.

Inspector Quirk: A veteran foot soldier of Scotland Yard, HE is a "gumshoe" of the old school, efficient in his work and, alas, officious in his demeanor.

Mrs. Mordant: A hard-bitten harridan, to whom life has been unkind, SHE is the housekeeper at HYDE'S Soho residence and a reluctant witness at the trial.

SCENE: JEKYLL'S laboratory, a mythical court room, and other locations around London.

TIME: Throughout the year of 1892.

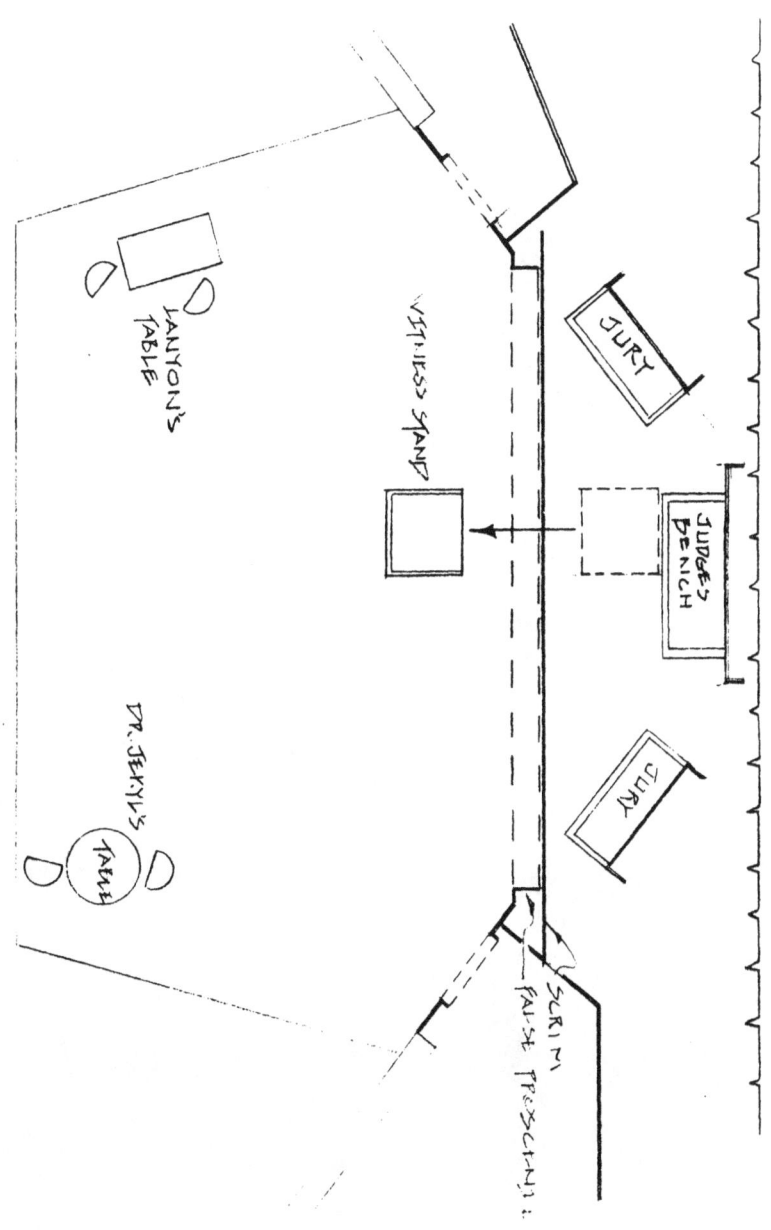

Designer Lee Lyons' floor plan for the initial production at California State University, San Bernardino, 1993.

ACT ONE

SETTING: The play is set in London in the early 1890's. There is a small writing desk and two chairs down stage left. On the desk are writing materials and a drinking glass containing a bluish liquid. The remainder of the stage is empty at rise. Later, a fantasy court room appears. Furniture pieces and properties can be added as needed.

AT RISE: The stage is dark. A strange, throbbing, discordant SOUND begins softly, rises in volume, and then subsides to a low whir under the recorded voice of a weakened JEKYLL.

VOICE. These will be the last words of Henry Jekyll. As I sit in my laboratory on this thirty-first day of December, 1892, I am overwhelmed by a feeling of horror; yet, I am also struck with a remarkable sense of relief. The events of the past year have enveloped me like some awful ectoplasm, which will shortly determine my fate for good and all, a fate that is chillingly irreversible.

(LIGHTS up slowly on JEKYLL at the writing desk, recording HIS last statement and confession. JEKYLL and his recorded VOICE begin to overlap.)

JEKYLL and VOICE. If it were in my power to change this course, I would do so with all the energy at my disposal.

(SOUND of rapping at a distant door.)

JEKYLL. But now, in these few minutes left to me, the time has come for one last look into the past.

(JEKYLL pauses and looks up. In the following, HE gradually leaves HIS writing and begins to address HIS remarks directly to the audience.)

JEKYLL. I am compelled by every righteous member that I possess to resolve once and for all, not only for myself but for those who remain to read this statement, the question that has been haunting my every thought: *(rising)* What are the limits to one's exploration beyond the depths of normal human knowledge? What is the balance here? Where is the guilt? And what of me?

(The figure of the QUESTIONER fades into view. HE is dressed like and has all the appearance of JEKYLL.)

JEKYLL. Can I defend my own intervention into the workings of natural order? I must find an answer before I close these unhappy pages. I must determine the moral truth that lies within all this.

(SOUND of a pounding gavel is heard, followed by the voice of the QUESTIONER. There is never an appearance of JEKYLL noticing the presence of the QUESTIONER.)

QUESTIONER. What is your full name?
JEKYLL. Henry Jekyll.
QUESTIONER. Your profession?
JEKYLL. Doctor of medicine.
QUESTIONER. And your age?
JEKYLL. My birth was on January 30, 1850. That makes me forty-two.
QUESTIONER. What was your station?
JEKYLL. I was raised in all the conveniences that wealth allows.
QUESTIONER. Think carefully, Dr. Jekyll: do you consider yourself a good man?

ACT ONE 3

(Crescendo of SOUND as LIGHTS go up on the suggestion of an English court room, which materializes around JEKYLL, styled somewhat surrealistically, with manikins as judge and jury. JEKYLL crosses and stands in the witness box.)

QUESTIONER. Let me repeat the question. Do you look upon yourself as a man of high character?

JEKYLL. *(with no hesitation)* To be sure. I am inclined by nature to industry, fond of the respect of the wise, and, I think, held in esteem by my fellow man.

QUESTIONER. Admirable traits. And yet, sir, it has been revealed to me that you were not always so attentive to the straight and narrow.

JEKYLL. What?

QUESTIONER. The straight and narrow, sir.

JEKYLL. Oh, ... yes. ... I don't deny it.

QUESTIONER. Aha!

JEKYLL. Still, the worst of my faults was a certain inpatient gaiety of disposition.

QUESTIONER. Which means you were somewhat of a roister, does it not?

JEKYLL. *(evasively)* I am not sure I understand your meaning.

QUESTIONER. *(irritated)* Damn it, man, you were, I take it, fond of an occasional cup?

JEKYLL. *(with hesitation)* Yes.

QUESTIONER. And you were want to mingle freely with women?

JEKYLL. *(again, evasively)* I see nothing wrong in that.

QUESTIONER. With women of a questionable nature. *(JEKYLL does not respond.)* Dr. Jekyll, sir, I am waiting for your answer.

JEKYLL. *(cautiously)* I will admit that in my youth I was predisposed to seek the company of women one might call high-livers, perhaps even of the wild sort. Yes, I ... I concede that.

QUESTIONER. Would you consider yourself a religious man?

JEKYLL. Not in the strict sense.

QUESTIONER. Meaning?

JEKYLL. There is in my mind a conflict between being a man of religion and a man of science. I, sir, consider myself the latter.

QUESTIONER. I see.

JEKYLL. That does not mean, however, that I do not hold to the principals of righteousness. I endeavor in both my personal and professional life to do what I can for others and, in so doing, set an example that will draw admiration and respect from those around me and from those I diligently serve in carrying out my medical duties.

QUESTIONER. *(pressing)* In so stating, do you see no inconsistency with the sporting life you have previously admitted to?

JEKYLL. No, sir.

QUESTIONER. "No, sir?" Come now, Dr. Jekyll. You see nothing in your past recklessness that conflicts with the image of respectability you so ardently attempt to convey?

JEKYLL. We are all born with a duality of nature, sir, with an ability toward both good and evil. It is the struggle in us all to subvert the one for the benefits of the other.

ACT ONE 5

QUESTIONER. Well, well, well! If I hear you correctly, sir, it is your contention that there is a bit of the old Satan in me? In our honored judge here? In the most pious man of the cloth?

JEKYLL. Decency is ephemeral, sir.

QUESTIONER. *(surprised)* You would go that far?

JEKYLL. I would go further and say the average man's mind is structured for evil. It is our lifelong quest, then, to overcome it, to smother it, to cage it, as it were.

QUESTIONER. And have you done so, sir?

JEKYLL. *(emphatically)* I am confident that I have. Yes, I have done more. I have celebrated the compassionate side of my nature, as can be confirmed by those who know me. Yes, I avow that Henry Jekyll has, in his mature years, overcome his wantonness and has steadfastly held to principals that are considered admirable by those of culture and intelligence.

(JEKYLL crosses away, addressing the audience, as the LIGHTS go down on the witness box.)

JEKYLL. Hence it came about that I concealed my pleasures; and that when I reached the years of reflection, and began to look around me and take stock of my progress and position in the world, I stood already committed to a profound duplicity of life, obsessed with the desire to embrace not only the rewards of accomplished good, but the sensual gratifications of my baser self. I hid such irregularities as I was guilty of, I hid them with an almost morbid sense of shame. And yet, both sides of me were in dead earnest. I was no more myself when I laid aside restraint and plunged headlong into degradation, than when I labored at the furtherance of knowledge or the relief of sorrow and suffering. Am I so different from others, then, in this regard? Do we not all fall prey to the darker elements within us? Or is there redemption in the separation of these two powers that we possess, these powers of good and evil. It chanced that the direction of my scientific studies, which led wholly towards the mystic and the transcendental, shed strong light on this awareness of the perennial war within me. With every day, I thus drew steadily nearer to the dictum: that man is not truly one, but verily two.

(JEKYLL sits at HIS desk and continues writing. LIGHTS fade down on HIM and up on the witness box, where ENFIELD is standing.)

QUESTIONER. Mr. Enfield, if you would please, relate to us the events of January last, the sixth of that month, to be exact.

ENFIELD. Yes, the sixth. Well, sir, ... let me see ... I had been to a *fete* for a prominent member of London--some place at the end of the world--and was on my way home, about three o'clock of a black winter morning.

QUESTIONER. You were on foot?

ENFIELD. Yes. I am quite accustomed to walking; as a matter of fact, I find it most enjoyable. I maintain no vehicle myself; and, of course, there were no public conveyances about at that early hour.

QUESTIONER. Had you been imbibing, sir?

ENFIELD. No, sir, I made no stops on the way.

QUESTIONER. But at the party, the *fete*, as you called it, you had nothing to drink of a ... toxic nature?

ACT ONE

ENFIELD. Well, I suppose I had a glass of dinner wine and an after-thought of good brandy, just the usual thing.

QUESTIONER. But nothing that would impair your vision or your memory of the events you are about to relate?

ENFIELD. Oh, not in the least. I pride myself in being one who carries such acts of civility in a manner expected of a gentleman. I was not, in the farthest reaches of comprehension, what you could call "ill effected" by the liquors. No. No, my senses were stimulated, enlivened by the briskness of the morning air.

QUESTIONER. Yes, well, now that we have that out of the way, go on with your story, if you will.

ENFIELD. Let me see. *(pausing to be precise)* Yes ... yes. My route home lay through a part of town where there was nothing to be seen but lamps.

QUESTIONER. Lamps, sir?

ENFIELD. Lamps. Street after street, and all the folks asleep; street after street, all lighted up as if for a procession and all as empty as a church.

QUESTIONER. Thank you. Now that you have set the scene, Mr. Enfield, would you please get to the action.

ENFIELD. Yes, of course... Yes, well, now then ... uh ... *(feeling the pressure of interrogation)* ... all at once I saw two figures: one, a small man who was stumping along at a good walk; and the other, a girl of eight or ten who was running as hard as she was able down a cross street *(with a glance around the court room).*

QUESTIONER. You saw two figures approaching from different directions. Yes, go on.

ENFIELD. Well sir, the two ran into one another naturally enough at the corner; and then came the horrible part of the thing; *(showing the effects of memory)* for the man trampled calmly over the child's body and left her screaming on the ground.

(LIGHTS out on the witness box and up on JEKYLL at his desk.)

JEKYLL. It was on the moral side, and in my own person, that I learned to recognize the thorough and primitive duality of man. And from an early date, even before the course of my scientific discoveries had begun to suggest the most naked possibility of such a miracle, I had learned to dwell with pleasure on the thought of the segregation of these elements. If each, I told myself, could be housed in distinct identities, life would be relieved of all that was unbearable. The unjust might go his way, delivered from the aspirations and remorse of his more upright twin; and the just could walk steadfastly and securely on his upward path, doing the good things in which he found his pleasure, and no longer exposed to disgrace and penitence by the hands of this other side of his nature, this extraneous evil. *(with great conviction)* It is the curse of mankind that these incongruous beings are thus bound together. How, then, could they be separated?

(LIGHTS down on JEKYLL and up on the witness box.)

QUESTIONER: Without any rhyme or reason, the brute threw the child to the ground?
ENFIELD: *(incensed)* It was hellish to see. It wasn't like a man, it was like a damned Juggernaut *(checking to see his effect on the room).*
QUESTIONER. Go on.

ACT ONE

ENFIELD. Well, sir, I gave a shout to summon help, took to my heels and collared my gentleman friend.

QUESTIONER. Bravo, Mr. Enfield. Well done.

ENFIELD. Thank you, sir.

QUESTIONER. Was there anyone else about at that hour of the morning?

ENFIELD. Well, I should say! The child's screams brought a crowd, including the parents; and soon a doctor appeared. Surprisingly, there was quite a hubbub for that black time of day.

QUESTIONER. And the culprit you so diligently apprehended, how did he react?

ENFIELD. He was perfectly cool, I must say, and made no resistance; but he gave me one look so ugly that it brought out the sweat on me as if I had been running a mile.

QUESTIONER. What was the condition of the child?

ENFIELD. Oh, she was not much the worse, more frightened according to the sawbones. And that, you might suppose, would be an end to it. But there was one curious circumstance.

QUESTIONER. Yes?

ENFIELD. I had taken a loathing to my gentleman at first sight. So had the child's family, which was only natural. But the doctor's case was what struck me.

QUESTIONER. How do you mean?

ENFIELD. Well, he was the usual cut and dried apothecary, of no particular age and color, with a strong Edinburgh accent, and about as emotional as a bagpipe *(laughing)*.

QUESTIONER. A bagpipe. Yes, yes, we get your meaning.

ENFIELD. *(sobering)* Well, sir, he was like the rest of us; every time he looked at my prisoner, I noticed the sawbones turn sick with the desire to kill him.

QUESTIONER. Really?

ENFIELD. I knew what was in his mind, just as he knew what was in mine; and killing being out of the question, we did the next best thing. Damned bully!

(LIGHTS out on the witness box and up on JEKYLL at HIS desk.)

JEKYLL. From my laboratory table I managed to compound a drug by which the natural powers of my spirit could be dethroned from their supremacy, and a second form and countenance substituted, none the less natural to me because they were the expression and bore the stamp of lower elements in my soul. I hesitated long before I put this theory to the test of practice. I knew well that I risked death; for any drug that so potently controlled and shook the very fortress of identity, might by the least scruple of an overdose utterly blot out that natural side of me which I looked to it to change. But the temptation of a discovery so singular and profound at last overcame the suggestions of alarm.

(A low rumbling SOUND of foreboding rises in the background.)

JEKYLL. I purchased at once, from a firm of wholesale chemists, a large quantity of a particular salt which I knew from my experiments to be the last ingredient required; *(rising and reliving the experience that follows.)* and late one accursed night I compounded the elements, watched them boil

ACT ONE

and smoke together in the glass, and when the ebullition had subsided, *(pantomimes drinking the liquid)* with a strong glow of courage, drank the potion. The most racking pangs ensued: a grinding in the bones, deadly nausea, and a horror of the spirit that cannot be exceeded at the hour of birth or death. Then these agonies began swiftly to subside, and I came to myself as if out of a great sickness. There was something strange in my sensations, something indescribably new and, from its very novelty, incredibly sweet. *(beginning to turn into HYDE)* I felt younger, lighter, happier in body. Within, I was conscious of a heady recklessness, a loosening of the bonds of obligation, an unknown but not an innocent freedom of the soul. *(and now gradually growing more evil in aspect, as his body takes on a contorted appearance)* I knew myself, at the first breath of this new life, to be more wicked, tenfold more wicked, sold a slave to my original evil; and the thought, in that moment, braced and delighted me like wine. I stretched out my hands, enjoying in the freshness of these new sensations; and in the act, I suddenly was aware that my stature, my whole being had become ... **bizarre**.

(The transformation to HYDE is now complete. There is a thunderous SOUND, followed by a piercing scream of a child. HYDE crosses to an imaginary door as ENFIELD leaves the witness box and rushes to HIM.)

ENFIELD. Stop! Damned bully! Damn you! What kind of a cad are you, bowling over a small child that way?

HYDE. *(cowering and shielding his face with his hat)* I am sorry to have inconvenienced.

ENFIELD. Inconvenienced! I should strangle you senseless. What is your name? Come on now, out with it, your name.

HYDE. Why, Hyde, sir, Mr. Edward Hyde.

ENFIELD. *(grabbing HYDE by the collar)* Sir, I intend to make a scandal for you. I shall cause a stink from one end of London to the other. If you have any friends or any credit, you shall lose them.

HYDE. *(bristling, ready to explode, then thinking better of it)* Well, if you choose to make capital out of this, I am naturally helpless. But let's not be hasty, my good man; let's talk about this matter, one gentleman to another. Perhaps we can avoid a scene. Name your price.

ENFIELD. *(releasing him)* Well, that's blunt indeed. No beating around the bush for you I see.

HYDE. There are measures to be considered here, beneficial to us both. Uh ... name your figure, sir, and let's make a settlement.

ENFIELD. Alright, if that's your game, here it is: restitution of one hundred pounds to the child's family and the incident will be forgotten by me and, I assure you, by the others.

HYDE. Oh, come now, that's a bit steep, is it not? Come, come, sir, be reasonable; let us say fifty pounds and call it a day.

ENFIELD. You heard what I said, *(grabbing him by the shirt collar again)* one hundred pounds, or you shall be in the hands of the police within the hour.

HYDE. I'm afraid you hold the high cards; ... yes indeed, yes indeed.

ENFIELD. Well, what's your answer?

ACT ONE 13

HYDE. Well, so be it. Wait here, sir, I shall return at once with the amount.

(HYDE quickly disappears through a door. LIGHTS out on the scene and up on the witness box, as ENFIELD returns to it.)

QUESTIONER. Well, that is peculiar, I must say. You had him in your grasp and you let him get away? He walked away, just like that?
ENFIELD. Yes, you might say so. He whipped out a key and entered a nearby building. Damn that man! If I wasn't a gentleman, I would have strangled the blackguard.
QUESTIONER. And then what happened?

(HYDE re-enters as LIGHTS go up on HIM.)

HYDE. I have the settlement, sir. *(with a hissing sound)* The account is now paid in full and the matter done with. Shall we shake on it to bind the bargain?
ENFIELD. Presently, he returned with the sum of ten pounds in gold and a check for the balance at Coutt's Bank, drawn payable to the bearer and signed with the name of ... Henry Jekyll.
QUESTIONER. But a man does not, in real life, walk into a door in the early hours of the morning and come out with another man's check for nearly a hundred pounds.
ENFIELD. I said as much.
HYDE. *(with an evil sneer)* Set your mind at rest, my good man; I will stay with you till the banks open and cash the check myself.

(LIGHTS go slowly out on HYDE.)

ENFIELD. Yes, I said as much; but when the bank opened its doors, I went in and gave the check to the cashier, telling him that I had every reason to believe it was a forgery.

QUESTIONER. And was it?

ENFIELD. Not a bit of it. The check was genuine.

QUESTIONER. Hmm.

ENFIELD. I see you feel as I do. Yes, it's a bad story, for this man was a fellow that nobody could have to do with, a really damnedable villain; and Jekyll is a man of the very pink of proprieties, celebrated, and one of your fellows who do what they call good.

QUESTIONER. Then how did you justify it?

ENFIELD. Blackmail, I called it, an honest man paying through the nose for some of the capers of his youth. Though, even that, was far from explaining it all.

QUESTIONER. And the building into which this Hyde ventured, was that Dr. Jekyll's residence?

ENFIELD. *(with a slight laugh)* Not likely, sir, a place of that nature.

QUESTIONER. And you never asked?

ENFIELD. No, sir, I have a delicacy about putting questions. I make it a rule of mine: the more it looks like Queer Street, the less I ask. So there it is.

QUESTIONER. Can you give us a description of Mr. Hyde?

ENFIELD. Well, sir, he is not easy to describe. There was something wrong with his appearance, something displeasing, something downright detestable.

ACT ONE

QUESTIONER. How do you mean?

ENFIELD. I never saw a man I so disliked, and yet I scarce know why. He gave a strong feeling of deformity, although I couldn't specify the point. He was an extraordinary looking man, and yet I really can name nothing out of the way. No, sir, I can make no hand of it nor can I describe him.

QUESTIONER. Did you tell anyone of this encounter, the police, anyone?

ENFIELD. Only a friend and kinsman of mine.

QUESTIONER. And that would be?

ENFIELD. A Mr. John Utterson.

QUESTIONER. How did that come about?

ENFIELD. Well, you see it is our custom to go for Sunday walks together. We put great store in these excursions, looking forward to them ... well, as jewels on the crown of good fellowship.

QUESTIONER. *(chuckling slightly)* Mr. Enfield, I find that almost poetic. Please continue.

ENFIELD. This particular walk took us down a by-street in a busy quarter of London. Quite unexpectedly we came to a two-story building I recognized. This was the place, sir, into which Edward Hyde had entered.

QUESTIONER. Can you describe the building?

ENFIELD. Well, sir, it was ... a plain-fronted affair with no windows, simply a door on the street level ... and, if I may say so, it bore the marks of prolonged and sordid negligence. Mark it now, that door is clearly connected in my mind with this very strange affair.

(LIGHTS go up on UTTERSON, peering at JEKYLL'S doorway.)

UTTERSON. Indeed, and what affair is that?
ENFIELD. And then I revealed the unpleasant event of two weeks earlier.
UTTERSON. And it was through this door you say?

(ENFIELD crosses to UTTERSON. LIGHTS out on the witness box.)

ENFIELD. That very door.
UTTERSON. Are you quite certain this is the building?
ENFIELD. There's no doubt about it.
UTTERSON. You haven't confused the streets?
ENFIELD. My dear John, there's no mistaking this building.
UTTERSON. Strange. *(aware that this is JEKYLL'S building)* But there's one point I want to ask: the name of the man who walked over the child.
ENFIELD. The blackguard's name? ... Well, I can't see what harm it can do. Hyde, it was, a Mr. Edward Hyde.
UTTERSON. Ah, Hyde, you say. I see. You are quite sure?
ENFIELD. I couldn't be more certain.
UTTERSON. And the one who endorsed the check?
ENFIELD. Oh, come now, he's a man well placed in this town and better to go unnamed, if you'll forgive me.
UTTERSON. Of course. Are you quite convinced he used a key, this Hyde?
ENFIELD. My dear sir--
UTTERSON. Yes, I know, it must seem strange. The fact is, I do not press you for the name of the other party

ACT ONE 17

because I know it already. You see, Richard, your tale has struck home.

ENFIELD. Really! Well, I think you might have warned me.

UTTERSON. But I caution you, if you have been inexact in any point, you had better correct it.

ENFIELD. But I have been pedantically **exact**, as you call it. The fellow had a key; and what's more he has it still. I saw him use it not a week ago. Yes, I came back to this place, intrigued by the incident. Standing in the alcove of a building across the street, I watched as he produced the key and ushered himself unceremoniously through that door.

UTTERSON. I see.

ENFIELD. *(There is a moment of silence.)* Well, yes. So that's the end of the matter. I'm ashamed of my long tongue. Let's be prudent and make a bargain never to refer to this again.

UTTERSON. Yes. Yes, with all my heart.

(The two MEN shake hands. LIGHTS out on ENFIELD and UTTERSON and up on JEKYLL, sitting at HIS desk.)

JEKYLL. With that first transformation to Hyde, I was conscious of no repugnance, for this, too, was myself. It seemed natural and human, yes, more single in nature, free from the ambiguities of duality. Later, I observed that when I wore the semblance of Edward Hyde, none could come near me at first without a visible misgiving. This, as I take it, was because all human beings, as we meet them, are commingled out of good and evil; and Edward Hyde, alone in the ranks of mankind, was pure evil. The second and conclusive experiment had yet to be attempted; it yet remained to be seen if I had lost my identity beyond redemption. I once more prepared and drank the cup, once more suffered the pangs of dissolution, and came to myself once more with the character, the stature, and the face of Henry Jekyll. The drug had no discriminating action; it was neither diabolical nor divine. *(with foreboding)* But it shook the doors of the prison-house of my disposition; and like the captives of Philippi, that which stood within ran forth; and alas! as I have in consequence discovered, the movement was thus wholly toward the worse.

(HIS words are punctuated by an eerie SOUND. LIGHTS out on JEKYLL and up on UTTERSON in the witness box.)

QUESTIONER. So, Mr. Utterson, you knew the names of the parties involved.

UTTERSON. Oh, yes.

QUESTIONER. And this aforementioned door into which Hyde disappeared?

UTTERSON. The rear entrance to Dr. Henry Jekyll's laboratory.

QUESTIONER. *(somewhat surprised)* I see. But you did not mention that to Enfield.

UTTERSON. No. I felt it was better to be discrete in the matter.

QUESTIONER. You say you knew Mr. Hyde?

UTTERSON. No, only by mention.

QUESTIONER. I see. And when was that?

UTTERSON. Approximately a year ago.

QUESTIONER. Go on.

UTTERSON. Dr. Jekyll had summoned me to his home to discuss his will.

ACT ONE 19

QUESTIONER. You are his solicitor?

UTTERSON. Yes, sir, and have been for some years.

QUESTIONER. Alright, go on. You went to Jekyll's lodgings--

UTTERSON. On this occasion I was ushered by Poole, Jekyll's head man, into the study. Immediately, the doctor opened a large safe and produced a document he had prepared for me, the contents of which were to serve as a codicil to his will.

QUESTIONER. And the contents?

UTTERSON. As I perused the paper I became quite disturbed, for it read to the effect that: in case of the decease of Henry Jekyll, all his possessions were to pass into the hands of--and this is a direct quote--"his friend and benefactor, Edward Hyde."

QUESTIONER. And do you have the document?

UTTERSON. I do. *(taking the document from his pocket)*

QUESTIONER. Would you read it quickly to be certain?

(UTTERSON peruses the paper quickly, then begins reading it aloud as HE crosses into the scene with JEKYLL. LIGHTS up on the scene and out on the witness box.)

UTTERSON. "... or in case of my disappearance or unexplained absence for any period exceeding three calendar months, Edward Hyde will assume my position without further delay and free from any burden or obligation, beyond the payment of a few small sums to the members of my household." *(putting down the paper)* My dear, Jekyll, this is absolutely perplexing.

JEKYLL. How so? The writing is quite uncluttered and to the point.

UTTERSON. Who is this Edward Hyde, this "friend and benefactor" to whom you refer.

JEKYLL. *(passing it off)* Hyde is a protege of mine.

UTTERSON. How do you mean?

JEKYLL. He is a young man whom I have befriended, an intelligent young man, a man of good prospects.

UTTERSON. And you have **befriended** this Hyde as an act of charity? What is his background, his schooling?

JEKYLL. *(evading the questions)* See here, I don't wish to have to explain Hyde. Suffice to say, he exists and will assume my possessions and household when and if my own existence were to terminate.

UTTERSON. My dear friend, how long have we known each other?

JEKYLL. Why, the better part of twenty years I should guess.

UTTERSON. And in all that time, in all of our pleasant evenings together, I have never met your Mr. Hyde, nor have I heard his name referred to until this very moment. I find that most strange and, as I say, perplexing.

JEKYLL. I see nothing unusual about it. How could you expect to know all my friends.

UTTERSON. But the one person to whom you endow your entire estate?

JEKYLL. Even so.

UTTERSON. Will you allow me to meet and talk to Hyde.

JEKYLL. He is not here.

UTTERSON. I didn't expect he would be, no. May I have his address so that I might call on him? Or perhaps you

ACT ONE

would be so kind as to set up a meeting between us. Yes, that would be best.

JEKYLL. I will do no such thing.

UTTERSON. But, good Lord, why?

JEKYLL. I don't wish to intrude upon the privacy of my friend Hyde.

UTTERSON. But it is a matter of great concern to me as your solicitor. It is only proper that I try to protect you from any possible danger.

JEKYLL. *(irritated)* Sir, I am in no mood to have to defend myself. Please take the paper with you and see that it becomes a part of the other documents you have in your possession.

UTTERSON. Very well, but against my better judgment.

JEKYLL. *(with more warmth)* And, John, for the sake of friendship, let us agree to say no more on this matter.

UTTERSON. But, Harry ...

JEKYLL. *(quickly)* Please.

UTTERSON. *(stiffly)* As you wish. I bid you good day.

(UTTERSON crosses back to the witness box. LIGHTS remain on JEKYLL.)

JEKYLL. The new power that I possessed began to distract me from my life of study and my professional duties as a physician, tempting me more and more to assume the person of Hyde, until I fell slavery to it. I had but to drink the cup, to doff at once the body of my better self, and to assume, like a thick cloak, the person of Edward Hyde. Soon I began to make my preparations with the most studious care. I took and furnished a house for Hyde in Soho, and engaged as house-keeper a creature whom I well knew to be silent and unscrupulous. On the other side, I announced to my servants that a Mr. Hyde, whom I described, was to have full liberty and power. And I drew up my will, so that if anything befell me in the person of Dr. Jekyll, I could continue as Edward Hyde without pecuniary loss. And thus fortified, as I supposed, I began to delight in the strange immunities of my position.

(LIGHTS out on JEKYLL and up on UTTERSON in the witness box.)

UTTERSON: Let me say that, although I took charge of this business of the will, I was not a party to the making of it. It offended me both as a solicitor and as a lover of the sane and customary sides of life. I thought it was madness, and now I begin to fear it is a disgrace.
QUESTIONER. So what did you do about it?
UTTERSON. In a day or two I paid a visit to Dr. Westley Lanyon on Cavendish Square.
QUESTIONER. The distinguished physician?
UTTERSON. Yes, sir. We have been friends since our college days. I thought if anyone can shed light on this Hyde person it will be Lanyon. I suppose we must be the two oldest friends of Harry Jekyll.

(LIGHTS up on LANYON, pouring sherry from a decanter, and out on the witness box. UTTERSON crosses into the scene.)

LANYON. Yes, I suppose we are. But what of that? I see very little of him now.

ACT ONE   23

UTTERSON. Indeed? I thought you had a bond of common interest.

LANYON. We had, is more to the point. Henry Jekyll has become too fanciful for me.

UTTERSON. Too fanciful?

LANYON. Yes, since he began to go wrong. Though I continue to take an interest in him for old sake's sake, as they say. No, I have seen devilish little of him of late.

UTTERSON. You say "wrong?" How do you mean it?

LANYON. Since he started dabbling in that laboratory of his. Such unscientific balderdash would have estranged Damon and Pythias.

UTTERSON. Aha! You have differed on some scientific points then?

LANYON. Differed indeed! There is grave danger in the half-cocked experiments he performs in that place of his. There are things in this universe, sir, that we are not intended to know nor understand.

UTTERSON. Well, I have no such scientific passions-- except in the matter of conveyancing of course. But to the point of my visit: did you ever come across a protege of his--a young Hyde?

LANYON. Hyde? Hyde? No never. The name is a complete stranger. He must have come into the picture after our falling out. What is the importance of Mr. Hyde?

UTTERSON. Forgive me, but it is a professional matter of the greatest discretion, ...

(UTTERSON crosses to the witness box. LIGHTS go up there and out on LANYON.)

UTTERSON. ... but one on which I had hoped he might shed some light.

QUESTIONER. Did this strike you as peculiar?

UTTERSON. Beg pardon?

QUESTIONER. The fact that you and Lanyon have known Jekyll for years and yet he has never introduced either of you to Hyde or, indeed, never included Hyde in his group for social gatherings?

UTTERSON. Well, of course it did; but, as you have heard, Jekyll was always extremely vague, even mysterious in his references to that man. And his attitude did not invite prying. If I did not know Jekyll as I do, I would have suspected there was some--how shall I put it?--some untoward relationship between the two.

QUESTIONER. Aha!

UTTERSON. But, no! That is out of the question. Jekyll is a man of high principles and quite normal in that regard, ... if you get my meaning.

QUESTIONER. I do, sir, and I shall close my mind to any suggestion of such misconduct. Now then, your unfruitful conversation with Jekyll, did this lay the matter rest?

UTTERSON. Not on your life. I was plagued by the curiosity of the thing and by a professional concern for my client. From that time forward I began to haunt the street behind Jekyll's laboratory. If he be Mr. Hyde, I said to myself, I be Mr. Seek.

QUESTIONER. *(chuckling again)* I see.

UTTERSON. Yes, sir. Then one night about the hour of ten my patience was rewarded.

QUESTIONER. How so?

ACT ONE   25

UTTERSON. I became aware of an odd footstep drawing near. Shortly, a man rounded the corner and made straight for that door.

(LIGHTS up on HYDE as he enters and crosses the stage toward JEKYLL'S laboratory door. UTTERSON intercepts HIM. LIGHTS out on witness box.)

UTTERSON. Mr. Hyde, I think.

(A startling SOUND is heard, which continues softly under the dialogue)

HYDE. *(shrinking back with a hissing sound and looking away, momentarily frightened)* What? What? That is my name. What ... what is your business?
UTTERSON. I see you are going in.
HYDE. Well, what of it?
UTTERSON. I am an old friend of Jekyll's--Mr. Utterson of Gaunt Street--you must have heard my name.
HYDE. *(shielding his face with his hat)* Utterson? Perhaps I have. What has this to do with me?
UTTERSON. Well now, meeting you so conveniently, I thought you might admit me.
HYDE. *(taken by surprise)* Admit you?
UTTERSON. Yes, to see my old friend.
HYDE. You will not find Jekyll. *(with an impish attitude)* He is not home.
UTTERSON. I see.
HYDE. *(abruptly, as HE starts to leave)* So good day to you, sir.

UTTERSON. *(attempting to draw HYDE into conversation)* I understand you are a protege of his.

HYDE. See here, I have no time for busy-bodies. *(suddenly, but without looking up)* How did you know me?

UTTERSON. Look you, sir, will you be kind enough to let me see your face.

HYDE. My face? Why ... if you wish.

(HYDE hesitates, then turns with an air of defiance. The TWO stare at each other for a moment.)

HYDE. Are you satisfied, sir?

UTTERSON. Quite. Now I shall know you if we ever meet again. It may be useful.

(UTTERSON turns to leave, but is stopped as HYDE hooks the head of HIS cane in UTTERSON'S coat and draws HIM back.)

HYDE. *(with a reckless bravado)* Yes, it is as well we have met; and *apropos*, you shall have my address. *(handing UTTERSON his card)* And now, sir, *(menacingly placing his cane under UTTERSON'S chin)* you owe me an answer. How did you know me?

UTTERSON. By description.

HYDE. Whose description?

UTTERSON. We have friends in common.

HYDE. Common friends? Who might they be?

UTTERSON. *(testing)* Jekyll, for instance.

HYDE. *(angrily)* Jekyll! Jekyll never told you. That is a lie, sir! *(going into a rage)* A lie! a lie! a confounded lie!

(The SOUND rises up to a finish. HYDE disappears into the

ACT ONE   27

darkness. UTTERSON crosses to the witness box as the LIGHTS go up there and out on the scene.)

QUESTIONER. And quick as a flash he disappeared into the building?

UTTERSON. Yes. His manner was most frightening, most terrifying.

QUESTIONER. And that was the end of it?

UTTERSON. He was gone, almost like evaporating into the air.

QUESTIONER. Can you recall his appearance?

UTTERSON. Oh, yes indeed. Mr. Hyde was a pale-looking man ... and dwarfish ... and he gave an impression of deformity without any nameable malformation.

QUESTIONER. That seems to be a common impression.

UTTERSON. And, oh, he had a displeasing smile. Indeed, he bore himself with a sort of murderous mixture of timidity and boldness.

QUESTIONER. Would you recognize his voice if you were to hear it again?

UTTERSON. Unmistakably. Oh yes! he spoke with a husky, whispering and somewhat broken sound.

QUESTIONER. Can you recall anything else?

UTTERSON. There must be something else. There is something more, if I could find a name for it. God bless me, the man seemed hardly human! If I ever read Satan's signature upon a face, it was on the face of Hyde. Even this cannot account for the disgust, the fear, yes, the loathing I had for the man.

QUESTIONER. Now then, did you have any further conversation with Jekyll about him?

UTTERSON. I tried, sir. Oh, yes, I tried. In fact, I went round to Jekyll's house at once. I wasn't about to leave things as they were, not on your life.

(LIGHTS up on POOLE, out on the witness box. UTTERSON crosses into the scene.)

POOLE. Why, it's Mr. Utterson. Good evening, sir.

UTTERSON. Yes, yes, Poole, is Dr. Jekyll at home? I regret the hour, but I must speak with him.

POOLE. I'm sorry, sir, but Dr. Jekyll has gone out.

UTTERSON. May I ask where?

POOLE. I don't know, sir. He don't inform me of his whereabouts.

UTTERSON. And I suppose you have no idea when he will be returning?

POOLE. None, sir.

UTTERSON. *(HE starts to leave, then turns back.)* I saw Mr. Hyde go in by the old dissecting-room door, Poole. Is that right when Dr. Jekyll is from home?

POOLE. Perfectly right, sir; Mr. Hyde has a key.

UTTERSON. Your master seems to repose a great deal of trust in that man.

POOLE. Yes, sir, he do indeed. We have all orders to obey him.

UTTERSON. I don't think I ever met Mr. Hyde.

POOLE: Oh, dear no, sir. He never dines here. Indeed, we see very little of him on this side of the house; he always comes and goes by the laboratory.

UTTERSON. Do you know anything about the man?

POOLE. Nothing, sir.

UTTERSON. Yes, I see. Well, thank you, Poole, and good night.

ACT ONE

POOLE. Good night, Mr. Utterson.

(POOLE exits. UTTERSON is held in thought. LIGHTS up on the witness box as UTTERSON enters it; out on scene.)

UTTERSON. Poor Harry Jekyll!

QUESTIONER. Yes? What were you thinking?

UTTERSON. It was at that moment that I felt a cloud of misgiving, fearful for poor Jekyll: this Master Hyde, if he were studied, must have secrets of his own--black secrets, by the look of him. The horror of it; if he suspects the existence of a will, he may grow impatient to inherit.

QUESTIONER. Let me see now, Mr. Utterson, you have just revealed an attempt to talk with Dr. Jekyll and share your concerns about his relationship with Mr. Hyde, which concluded in Jekyll being out of the house. Were there any further such attempts?

UTTERSON. *(fondly recalling the occasion)* Indeed, yes. A fortnight later, by excellent good fortune, Harry gave one of his pleasant dinners to some five or six of us, all intelligent, reputable men, and all judges of good wine.

QUESTIONER. And it was an enjoyable affair, I should guess?

UTTERSON. Well, yes, much good fellowship, for he's an admirable host.

QUESTIONER. And Mr. Hyde was nowhere to be seen.

UTTERSON. Not at all.

QUESTIONER. *(jokingly)* Not hide nor hair, as they say.

UTTERSON. *(laughing reservedly)* That is correct. However, as the gathering was leaving, I stayed behind, hoping for an opportunity to express my concerns.

(LIGHTS out on the witness box and up on JEKYLL. UTTERSON crosses in. BOTH have empty sherry glasses. During the conversation, POOLE enters with a tray and collects them.)

UTTERSON A most enjoyable evening, Harry; but then, you always were the best of hosts at a dinner party.

JEKYLL. Must you leave so early?

UTTERSON. I'm afraid so. But before I do, I have been wanting to speak to you, about ... well, you know that will of yours?

JEKYLL. Oh, dear, not again.

UTTERSON. I am gravely concerned about it.

JEKYLL. *(laughing it off)* My poor Utterson, you are unfortunate in such a client. I'm sorry to cause you so much concern.

UTTERSON. I'm serious about this, Harry.

JEKYLL. I never saw a man so distressed as you are by my will; unless it were that pedant, Lanyon, at what he calls my scientific heresies. Oh, I know he's a good fellow--you needn't frown--an excellent fellow, and I always mean to see more of him; but, for all of that, an ignorant, blatant pedant.

UTTERSON. *(ignoring the latter)* You know I never approved of it.

JEKYLL. My will? *(sharply)* Yes, certainly, I know that; you've told me so.

UTTERSON. Well, I tell you so again. I have been learning something of your Mr. Hyde.

JEKYLL. *(paling)* I don't care to hear any more. This is a matter I thought we had agreed to drop.

ACT ONE 31

UTTERSON. What I heard was abominable.

JEKYLL. It can change nothing. You don't understand my position. It is a ... a very strange one. I am painfully situated, John. It is one of those things that cannot be mended by talking.

UTTERSON. Harry, you know me; I am a man to be trusted. I beg you, make a clean breast of this in confidence, and I have no doubt I can get you out of it.

JEKYLL. *(touched)* My dear Utterson, this is very good of you, downright good of you, and I can't find words to thank you. I would trust you before any man alive, aye, before myself, if I could make the choice. But, indeed, it isn't what you fancy. And just to put your heart at rest, I will tell you one thing: the moment I choose, I can be rid of Mr. Hyde. I give you my hand upon that, and I thank you again and again. *(And HE does.)* But I will just add one little word that I'm sure you will take in good part: this is a private matter and I beg you to let it sleep.

UTTERSON. *(with coolness)* I have no doubt you are perfectly right. *(beginning to leave)*

JEKYLL. Well, but since you have touched upon this business, and for the last time I hope, there is one point I should like you to understand. I have really a great concern for poor Hyde. I know you have seen him--he told me so--and I fear he was rude. But I take a very great interest in that young man; and if I by chance should die or disappear, I want you to promise me that you will bear with him and get his rights for him. As a friend, John? It will be a weight off my mind.

UTTERSON. I can't pretend that I will ever like him.

JEKYLL. I don't ask that. I only ask for justice; I only ask you to help him for my sake, when I am no longer here.

UTTERSON. *(reluctantly)* Well, I promise. *(HE exits.)*

JEKYLL. Men have before hired others to transact their crimes, while their own person and reputation sat under shelter. I was the first that ever did so for his pleasures. I was the first that could thus walk in the public eye, wearing the mask of genial respectability, and in a moment, strip it off and spring headlong into the sea of liberty. For me, the safety was complete. Think of it--I did not even exist! Let me but escape into my laboratory, give me but a second or two to mix and swallow the draught that I had always standing ready; and whenever he was done, Edward Hyde would pass away like the stain of breath upon a mirror; and there in his stead, quietly at home, trimming the midnight lamp in his study--a man who could afford to laugh at suspicion--would be Henry Jekyll. The pleasures which I made haste to seek in my disguise were of the most sordid sort that men with the most voracious appetites can lay claim to. Hyde's savagery with women--that is, women hired for sport--is still painful to contemplate. Yet, such sexual aberrations allowed Jekyll to pursue a life of admirable celibacy. When I would come back from these excursions, I was often plunged into a kind of wonder at my vicarious depravity. Henry Jekyll stood at times aghast before the acts of Edward Hyde. It was Hyde, after all, and Hyde alone, that was guilty. Jekyll was no worse; he woke again to his good qualities seemingly unimpaired; he would even make haste, where it was possible, to undo the evil done by Hyde. *(JEKYLL sits at HIS desk and writes out this last remark.)* And thus my conscience slumbered.

(There is a sudden SOUND similar to a clap of thunder.

ACT ONE 33

LIGHTS dim lower on JEKYLL and up on the witness box, where POOLE is standing.)

QUESTIONER. Now then, Mr. Poole, you are in the employ of Dr. Henry Jekyll. Is that true?

POOLE. Yes, sir.

QUESTIONER. For how long?

POOLE. Beg pardon, sir?

QUESTIONER. How long have you been a member of Dr. Jekyll's household staff?

POOLE. Why, the larger part of ten years I should guess.

QUESTIONER. Would you say, then, that you are a trusted employee?

POOLE. I hope that is the case, sir; and I believe it to be so. I have the responsibility of running the house--*carte blanche*, as they say, sir--and, in all the years I have attended him, Dr. Jekyll has never suggested that my services were unsatisfactory.

QUESTIONER. Does that mean, Poole, that he confides in you?

POOLE. Oh, glory! no, sir. He does not, and indeed I don't expect it. That's not a part of my job. I have no desire to be burdened down with confidential matters.

QUESTIONER. Do you know a man by the name of Edward Hyde?

POOLE. I know of him.

QUESTIONER. Is he a member of your household?

POOLE. Oh, no, sir.

QUESTIONER. Mr. Hyde does not reside there?

POOLE. No, sir.

QUESTIONER. Have you ever seen him there?

POOLE. Oh, yes, often.
QUESTIONER. How often.
POOLE. Well, it varies. I don't know. It's not one's job to keep count.
QUESTIONER. But would you say that Mr. Hyde visits Jekyll's home once a month, once a week, twice a week, what?
POOLE. Begging your pardon, but it's hard to say, sir. I'm not always aware of when he visits. He used to come quite infrequently, but over the past year his appearances have increased, from what I've been able to observe.
QUESTIONER. As much as twice a week?
POOLE. Perhaps. You see, it's difficult to judge; he never comes into my side of the house. He always remains in the laboratory, coming in from the back ... except ...
QUESTIONER. Yes?
POOLE. Well, there was one time ...
QUESTIONER. Yes, Poole, you have something in mind?
POOLE. Well, one morning I saw him come out of Dr. Jekyll's bedroom.
QUESTIONER. Jekyll's bedroom?
POOLE. Yes, sir.

(LIGHTS go up on JEKYLL at his desk.)

JEKYLL. *(to HIMSELF at his table)* Yes, I had gone to bed Harry Jekyll and I had awakened Edward Hyde.
QUESTIONER. What hour of the morning?
JEKYLL. "How was this to be explained?" I asked myself.
POOLE. Oh, I can't recall to the minute, but I would say it was around seven.
QUESTIONER. Didn't you find that strange, since he never appeared in that side of the house?

ACT ONE 35

POOLE. Well, ... yes, ... I did think it a bit odd, but it isn't my business to question, sir.

QUESTIONER. So Hyde came out of Jekyll's bedroom, eh, Poole? How did he appear? Describe his behavior.

POOLE. He ignored me, acted as if I wasn't there, looking away all the while. I said, "Can I be of service, sir?" But he paid no heed, just rushed past me and in through the laboratory door.

JEKYLL. *(writing)* This incident, this reversal of my previous experience, seemed to be a signal of foreboding.

QUESTIONER. And that was the only occasion you have encountered him coming from Jekyll's bed chambers?

POOLE. It's the only occasion I've had need to speak to him at all, sir.

(LIGHTS out on witness box.)

JEKYLL. That part of me which I had the power of projecting, had lately been much exercised and nourished; it had seemed to me of late as if the body of Edward Hyde had grown in stature, as though (when I wore that form) I was conscious of a more generous tide of blood; and I began to spy a danger that, if this were much prolonged, the balance of my nature might be permanently overthrown, the power of voluntary change be forfeited, and the character of Edward Hyde become irrevocably mine. *(rising)* In the light of that morning's accident, I was led to observe that, whereas, in the beginning, the difficulty had been to throw off the body of Jekyll, it had of late gradually but decidedly transferred itself to the other side. All things therefore seemed to point to this: that I was losing hold of my original and better self, and becoming slowly incorporated with my second and worse.

(Repeat of the thunder-like SOUND. LIGHTS out on JEKYLL, up on witness box.)

QUESTIONER. Where is the witness? Will the witness

please come forward. Is there a Miss Gillian in the room? *(searching the audience)* Where is she? She was supposed to appear today. Is there a Miss Gilliam here?

(GILLIAN slowly rises from one of the seats.)

    QUESTIONER. Are you the witness?
    GILLIAN. *(fearfully)* My name is Gillian, your honor.
    QUESTIONER. Didn't you hear your name called?
    GILLIAN. Yes, sir.
    QUESTIONER. You are called to the witness box.
    GILLIAN. *(without moving)* Yes, sir.
    QUESTIONER. Well, ... come forward.
    GILLIAN. Do I have to?
    QUESTIONER. Of course. You are required to testify. Now, stop wasting our time. We have to get on with this.
    GILLIAM. I'm afraid, sir.
    QUESTIONER. There's nothing to fear. You're not on trial. You're a witness, nothing more.

(GILLIAN slowly makes her way toward the witness box. Once there, SHE bursts into tears.)

    QUESTIONER. Oh, come now, madam. This won't get us anywhere. Try to compose yourself. We just want to hear about what you saw on the night in question. Just relax and respond as accurately as you can.
    MISS GILLIAN. *(trying to gain composure)* I'm a bit nervous, your honor. I've never had to do anything like this before. It gives me the holy jibbers, being in front of all these people.
    QUESTIONER. I understand. But don't worry; it will all

ACT ONE 37

be over in a few minutes. Now then, what is your occupation?

(GILLIAN is hypnotized by all the people in the court, as SHE stares from one face to another.)

QUESTIONER. Will the witness please answer the question? What is your occupation?
MISS GILLIAN. *(returing to reality)* I'm a maid servant to the Washburns, your honor. I keep the upstairs rooms.
QUESTIONER. Think back, if you will, to the night of October 10 of this year, the night of the dastardly crime.
MISS GILLIAN. Oh bless me, your honor, the thought of it sends me into shivers. I wish I could forget it all, upon my soul, I do. It's been the devil's curse to me. *(beginning to sob)* I haven't had a decent night's rest in all these months, I swear I haven't.
QUESTIONER. Yes, well, I know it is difficult, but try to calm your mind. As you know, this is extremely important. You are the sole witness of this matter.
MISS GILLIAN. *(startled)* What?
QUESTIONER. I said you are the only witness we have who can ...

(HE is interrupted as GILLIAN again bursts into noisy tears.)

QUESTIONER. Come now, Miss Gillian, I am not going to bite you. I am only going to ask you a few questions. Now try your best to cooperate. It will be most helpful to me, to us all. Just relax.
MISS GILLIAN. *(attempting to gain composure)* I'll do my best.
QUESTIONER. I am certain you will. Now then, tell us, if you can, how you happened to be at your bedroom window at such an opportune moment of this particular night, the night of October 10.

MISS GILLIAN. I had gone to my room to retire. My job is a taxing one, your honor; and my hours are long--too long, if you ask me.

QUESTIONER. *(getting a bit impatient)* Yes, yes, I can sympathize with you. Go on.

MISS GILLIAN. It is my custom, before going to bed, to sit in my chair, which is placed at the window and, there, look out upon the comings and goings in the street. It is restful to me. *(with a look at the QUESTIONER and around the room)*

QUESTIONER. Go on, Miss Gillian; you're doing splendidly.

MISS GILLIAN. I must admit I often dream I am one of them fancy-dressed ladies that pass by in their carriages, and I make up all kinds of stories in my mind about where I've been and the large and beautiful place I am driving home to. It's all I have, you see.

QUESTIONER. And on this night?

MISS GILLIAN. I can tell you, sir, I never felt more at peace or thought more kindly of the world, ... until ... *(beginning to tear)*

QUESTIONER. So you were at your window observing the night traffic in the street. Is that correct?

MISS GILLIAN. Yes, sir.

QUESTIONER. And what time was this?

MISS GILLIAN. About eleven o'clock.

QUESTIONER. Do you have a clear view from your window?

MISS GILLIAN. Oh, yes.

QUESTIONER. But it was eleven o'clock, you say? Was it not dark in the street at that hour?

MISS GILLIAN. Oh, no, your honor. The street is well lit by lamps; it is a part of London where many reputable and high-born people reside.

QUESTIONER. And was it a clear night?

MISS GILLIAN. Well, the fog did come in some hours later, but at this time when ... well, you know, when it

ACT ONE 39

happened, there was a full moon which lighted the street brighter than usual. Oh, I could see what happened all right. *(beginning to get distraught again)* I could see it too, too well. Oh, God help me, your honor, I wish I hadn't.

QUESTIONER. Was there much traffic at this hour?

MISS GILLIAN. Begging your pardon?

QUESTIONER. Were there many people in the street?

MISS GILLIAN. Not at this time. No, there was not a soul astir from either direction, ... until ... *(nodding knowingly to him)*

QUESTIONER. Yes, until then. Now, please tell us, to the best of your recollection, what you saw.

MISS GILLIAN. I became aware of an elderly gentleman approaching. I had seen him many times taking his exercise at this hour. He always impressed me with his pretty manners and his expression of kindness. *(looking for instructions)*

QUESTIONER. Go on, Miss Gillian.

MISS GILLIAN. Then, from the other direction, I saw someone else, a small, odd-looking man. "Here's one I had never seen before from my window; here's one who was a stranger to this street," I said to myself. *(looking for further instructions)*

QUESTIONER. Yes, please go on.

MISS GILLIAN. When they come within speech, which was just below my window, the younger one stopped, as if to ask directions.

QUESTIONER. You couldn't hear them converse from where you were?

MISS GILLIAN. Oh, no, your honor. But from the way the older man was looking and pointing, that seemed to be the case.

QUESTIONER. I see. And then?

MISS GILLIAN. The younger one appeared to get irritated and began waiving a heavy cane he was carrying and then broke out in an ungodly anger, stamping with his foot and carrying on like a madman. Oh, it was too awful, sir!

QUESTIONER. Yes, and how did the elderly man react to this commotion?

MISS GILLIAN. He stepped back and looked a deal surprised and a trifle hurt. And at that, the younger one broke out of all bounds and ... and ... *(beginning to cry)*

QUESTIONER. Yes, go on. I know it is difficult for you but you must tell us what happened.

MISS GILLIAN. ... and he clubbed him to the earth, again and again and again he hit him. Oh, dear God!

QUESTIONER. And then what happened, Miss Gillian?

MISS GILLIAN. The madman raised his head as if to the sky and began to laugh, a most terrifying sound, sir, a most blood-thirsty noise it was.

QUESTIONER. Then what did he do?

MISS GILLIAN. I don't know. I didn't see any more.

QUESTIONER. Did you run for help?

MISS GILLIAN. No, sir, I fainted. But I later learned he was dead; murdered, sir, murdered right before my eyes.

QUESTIONER. Alright, Miss Gillian, now we come to the most important part. When the man looked up and laughed, with the moonlight falling upon his face, did you see his countenance clearly?

MISS GILLIAN. Yes, your honor.

QUESTIONER. And did you recognize who he was?

MISS GILLIAN. Yes, your honor.

QUESTIONER. And who was this man?

MISS GILLIAN. He was a man who once visited my master.

QUESTIONER. Are you certain of that?

MISS GILLIAN. As God is holy, I couldn't forget that face.

QUESTIONER. His name, Miss Gillian, what was this man's name.

MISS GILLIAN. His name was Hyde, God save me, sir; yes, his name was Hyde. *(bursting into tears)*

ACT ONE 41

(SOUND of finality. LIGHTS out on witness box, up on JEKYLL.)

JEKYLL. The time came when I felt I had to make a choice. My two natures had memory in common, but all other faculties were most unequally shared between them. Jekyll projected a interest in the adventures of Hyde; but Hyde was indifferent to Jekyll. To cast in my lot with Jekyll was to die to those appetites which I had long secretly indulged and had of late begun to pamper. To cast it in with Hyde was to die to a thousand interests and aspirations, and to become, at a blow and forever, despised and friendless. Yes, well, I preferred the older and discontented doctor, surrounded by friends and cherishing honest hopes; and bade a resolute farewell to the liberty, the light step, leaping impulses and secret pleasures that I had enjoyed in the disguise of Hyde. I made this choice with some unconscious reservation, for I neither gave up the house in Soho nor destroyed the clothes of Edward Hyde, which still lay ready in my room. For two months I was true to my determination. I led a life of such severity as I had never before attained to, and enjoyed the compensations of an approving conscience. But then, time began at last to obliterate my resolution. I began to be tortured with throes of longings, and, at last, in an hour of moral weakness, I once again compounded and swallowed the transforming draught. My devil had long been caged; and now he came out roaring.

(SOUND of rage, followed by the sobs of GILLIAN. LIGHTS out on JEKYLL, up on scene.)

INSPECTOR QUIRK. Alright, Miss, stop the sobbing. Everything's being taken care of.

(GILLIAN continues. QUIRK looks helpless.)

INSPECTOR QUIRK. Miss, this is Inspector Quirk from Scotland Yard, here to look into this matter.

(That brings GILLIAN around.)

INSPECTOR QUIRK. Now then, what is your name?
MISS GILLIAN. My name is ... *(Again SHE bursts into tears.)*
INSPECTOR QUIRK. Damnit! young lady, will you stop that! How can I get to the bottom of this when you can't even answer a simple question? Now then, what is your name?
MISS GILLIAN. Louise, sir, Louise Gillian.
INSPECTOR QUIRK. You work here, is that right?
MISS GILLIAN. Yes, sir, the upstairs maid.
INSPECTOR QUIRK. And you were the one who called the police?
MISS GILLIAN. Yes, sir.
INSPECTOR QUIRK. And you were the witness to this bloody murder?
MISS GILLIAN. Yes, sir, God help me. *(SHE begins to cry again.)*
INSPECTOR QUIRK. Stop that and answer my questions! Carrying on will do no good at all.

(GILLIAN recovers.)

ACT ONE 43

INSPECTOR QUIRK. Now, what time was it that you saw this happen?

MISS GILLIAN. Around eleven, sir.

INSPECTOR QUIRK. My God, woman, it's three o'clock in the morning. What took you so long to summon help? The culprit's long gone by now.

MISS GILLIAN. I fainted, sir.

INSPECTOR QUIRK. Fainted!

(LIGHTS out on scene, up on witness boxas QUIRK crosses to it.)

QUESTIONER. Yes, she fainted.

INSPECTOR QUIRK. She fainted. God bless me, she was out for over three hours. No chance of catching this Hyde person that night and nowhere to look.

QUESTIONER. But the body was still in the street?

INSPECTOR QUIRK. I should say so, what was left of it. The poor fellow had been beaten unmercifully, over and over I must say, and trampled underfoot. The bones were shattered and the face and arms were a bloody mess. It wasn't a sight for the Queen to see, I can tell you that, sir.

QUESTIONER. The body was mangled and the man left to die. Is that correct?

INSPECTOR QUIRK. No, sir. The poor fellow must have died during the beating, from the looks of things.

QUESTIONER. And the weapon, did you find any trace of it?

INSPECTOR QUIRK. I did, sir, in the neighboring gutter, a piece of a stick, some rare and very tough and heavy wood, broken in the middle under the stress. The other half, without doubt, was carried away by the murderer.

QUESTIONER. The stick, leaning against the railing there, would that be the one?

INSPECTOR QUIRK. *(picking the stick up and looking it over)* It is indeed, sir; this is the very item.

QUESTIONER. What was the motive of this insensate cruelty would you say?

INSPECTOR QUIRK. Not robbery, sir. A purse and a gold watch were still on the victim.

QUESTIONER. And identification?

INSPECTOR QUIRK. None directly, no cards or papers, nothing except a letter, stamped and sealed, which he was probably carrying to the post.

QUESTIONER. Then it bore a name?

INSPECTOR QUIRK. A Mr. John Utterson.

QUESTIONER. Ah, Mr. Utterson.

INSPECTOR QUIRK. Yes, sir. I went round to his lodgings as quickly as a respectable hour allowed.

(LIGHTS up on a coatless UTTERSON.)

UTTERSON. I shall say nothing till I have seen the body. This may be very serious. Have the kindness to wait while I dress.

(UTTERSON disappears, but returns shortly with coat and hat.)

INSPECTOR QUIRK. He is a solicitor, you know, and weren't about to jump at anything hasty. So I took the gentleman down and showed him the body.

ACT ONE   45

(LIGHTS out on witness box. QUIRK, carrying the stick, crosses to UTTERSON.)

UTTERSON. *(aghast)* Yes, I recognize him. I am sorry to say that this is Sir Danvers Carew.

INSPECTOR QUIRK. Good God, sir, is it possible? This will make a deal of a noise, a man of his prominence.

UTTERSON. Yes, yes, a man loved and respected by all of London, yes, all of England. What a tragedy! His family must be notified.

INSPECTOR QUIRK. I'll take care of it, sir.

UTTERSON. Who would commit such a bestial thing?

INSPECTOR QUIRK. A madman, sir, a madman by the name of Hyde.

UTTERSON. *(taken aback)* Hyde you say? Is this Mr. Hyde a person of small stature?

INSPECTOR QUIRK. Particularly small and particularly wicked-looking is what the maid calls him.

UTTERSON. Good God, man, I know of this Hyde, and a madman indeed, to be able to so desecrate and mutilate a human body, no matter what its age. He must have unbelievable strength.

INSPECTOR QUIRK. He used this stick, sir, or the whole of it until it broke in two.

UTTERSON. Let me see it, Inspector. *(taking the stick from QUIRK)* God in heaven!

INSPECTOR QUIRK. What is it?

UTTERSON. I know this stick!

INSPECTOR QUIRK. What's that?

UTTERSON. Broken and battered as it is, I would know it anywhere. It is one that I presented years ago to my dear friend, Dr. Henry Jekyll.

(SOUND of uncontrolled lunacy, continuing under HYDE'S speech, then up for act finish. LIGHTS out on scene, up on JUDGE'S bench. HYDE has pushed the judge aside and is standing there, a picture undeniable evil.)

HYDE. The spirit of hell awoke in me and raged! With a transport of glee, I mauled the old man's body, delighting in every blow. Then I fled from the scene, my lust of evil gratified, my love of life screwed to the top-most peg. Thence I set out through the lamplit streets and hurried to Jckyll's place, gloating on my crime, devising others in the future. I had a song on my lips as I compounded the draught, and as I drank it, I pledged the dead man's health. *(HYDE concludes with a chilling laugh.)*

(SOUND of eerie laughter echos through the theatre as LIGHTS fade out. End of Act One.)

Top: "We are all born with a duality of nature, sir, with an ability toward good and evil. ..." (page 4)
Bottom: "Your master seems to repose a great deal of trust in that man." (page 28)

ACT TWO

AT RISE: The TIME is continuous from ACT ONE. The court room is still visible in the background. The MANNEQUINS are now postured in disarray. A table and two chairs have been added down right. The LIGHTS come up on JEKYLL at HIS desk.

JEKYLL. The murder of Sir Danvers Carew was not only a crime, it had been a tragic folly. I think I was glad to know it; I think I was glad to have my better impulses thus buttressed and guarded by the terrors of the scaffold. Jekyll was now my refuge. Let but Hyde peep out an instant, and the hands of all men would be raised to take and slay him. I resolved in my future conduct to redeem the past; and I can say with honesty that my resolve was fruitful of some good. A new life began for Dr. Jekyll. I came out of my seclusion, renewed relationships with my friends, became once more their familiar guest and entertainer. Whilst I had always been known for charities, I became now no less distinguished for religion. I was busy, I was much in the outdoors, I did good. My countenance became open and bright, and for two months I was at peace. The days passed quietly, almost happily for myself.

(JEKYLL pauses, somewhat blissfully, to contemplate this last statement. The silence is interrupted by the QUESTIONER'S voice. LIGHTS out on JEKYLL, up on witness box.)

QUESTIONER. So Mr. John Utterson knew the address of Hyde's lodgings?
INSPECTOR QUIRK. He did, sir.

(LIGHTS up on UTTERSON up left.)

UTTERSON. If you will come with me in my cab, I think I can take you to his house.

(LIGHTS dim down on UTTERSON while HE waits for QUIRK to join HIM.)

INSPECTOR QUIRK. He appeared to have a card given him by this Mr. Hyde. Now there's a foolish trick, I must say; a man of his criminal inclinations, giving his address to what one might call a stranger. But sometimes there's no accounting for the workings of a demented mind. I've seen it happen over and over again in my trade, sir.

QUESTIONER. And you went with Utterson to this Soho residence of Hyde's?

INSPECTOR QUIRK. You can bet on it.

QUESTIONER. When exactly was this?

INSPECTOR QUIRK. Why, the morning following the murder, sir. We waste no time in getting on these cases. No grass grows under Scotland Yard, as they say.

QUESTIONER. So you showed Mr. Utterson the body; and once he identified it, you went directly there.

INSPECTOR QUIRK. I wouldn't say directly. Not ... uh ... exactly. You see, it took us a while to find the place. By this time it was around nine in the morning and a heavy fog had rolled in.

QUESTIONER. But that didn't stop Scotland Yard, eh, no grass and all that?

INSPECTOR QUIRK. Oh, we don't let the weather detain us from our duty. No, sir. *(with a look as if awaiting a congratulatory response)*

QUESTIONER. Go on.

INSPECTOR QUIRK. Well, sir, to be sure, we had some difficulty finding the place. Our cab crawled from street to street, getting lost at times; but finally, you can depend on it, we ended up at the intended destination.

QUESTIONER. And this was the locale you were seeking?

INSPECTOR QUIRK. It was, indeed; the very locale, as you put it.

ACT TWO 49

QUESTIONER. An unseemly quarter of Soho I should guess.

INSPECTOR QUIRK. Oh, you can believe it. It was a dingy neighborhood alright, festering with all the evils of the city. I've known these places, sir. A criminal can come and go with no one taking notice. *(with an added bit of incite)* Now here's a point: as the cab came to a stop, I heard Utterson say ...

(LIGHTS up on UTTERSON.)

UTTERSON. So this is the home of a man who is heir to a quarter of a million sterling.

(UTTERSON remains, looking at HYDE'S residence.)

INSPECTOR QUIRK. I took note of it, you see, although it has no meaning. In my profession you don't let anything pass without tucking it away. That's the first rule of sleuthing. Yes, sir, I learned that early.
QUESTIONER. Thank you, Inspector Quirk, for the brief lesson. Then what happened?
INSPECTOR QUIRK. Well, sir, we knocked at the door and shortly it was opened by some hard-faced biddy. *(with a chuckle)* A face like granite, yes, sir. I've seen her kind before, smooth manners but a lie behind every expression.

(MRS. MORDANT enters up left and stands blocking the door. LIGHTS on the witness box. QUIRK crosses into the scene.)

MRS. MORDANT. Yes, this is Mr. Hyde's residence.
UTTERSON. We'd like to see him, if you please.
INSPECTOR QUIRK. I'm Inspector Quirk of Scotland Yard. *(showing his credentials)* and we're here to see Mr. Edward Hyde on some very important business.

MRS. MORDANT. Ah, he's in trouble, is he? *(appearing to enjoy it)*

INSPECTOR QUIRK. *(to UTTERSON)* He don't seem a very popular character.

MRS. MORDANT. What's he done?

INSPECTOR QUIRK. Never you mind what he's done. Let me repeat myself, madame: we're here to see Mr. Edward Hyde.

MRS. MORDANT. Well, you can't.

INSPECTOR QUIRK. Now, none of that. Just stand aside, if you please. There's no time to be wasted with the likes of you.

MRS. MORDANT. You can't see him 'cause he ain't in.

INSPECTOR QUIRK. Ah, gone out.

MRS. MORDANT. Well, if he ain't here, he must have gone out, now mustn't he.

UTTERSON. My good woman, this is not something for jest. We are here to talk to Mr. Hyde about a very important matter.

INSPECTOR QUIRK. That's right. So don't give us the edge of your tongue, m'lady. Just let me and this gentleman in and have a look about us.

MRS. MORDANT. I don't have instructions from the master to let strangers go tramping through the place. Come back when he's home.

INSPECTOR QUIRK. Now none of that. We're here on official business, about a matter of criminality, if you please. So stand aside and let the law take its course.

UTTERSON. Inspector, allow me.

(With a wave of disgust, QUIRK moves aside. UTTERSON removes his hat and confronts MRS. MORDANT with an exaggerated air of politeness.)

UTTERSON. It so happens, madame, this is important, and I assure you no harm will come to the place.

ACT TWO 51

(MORDANT stiffens and remains immovable. LIGHTS out on scene, up on the witness box as QUIRK moves to it.)

QUESTIONER. And so, Inspector, you had a look around?

INSPECTOR QUIRK. We did. We forced our way past the woman--a quite determined guardian she was, for all that.

QUESTIONER. Go on.

INSPECTOR QUIRK. Well, sir, in the whole of the house, Mr. Hyde had occupied only a few rooms.

QUESTIONER. Really?

INSPECTOR QUIRK. But these were furnished to the nines--like the sitting room of one your fancy hotels, they were.

QUESTIONER. Rather expensive trappings for Soho, wouldn't you say?

INSPECTOR QUIRK. I would say that, sir, I would indeed.

QUESTIONER. Then aside from the well-placed furnishings, there was nothing out of the ordinary within the dwelling?

INSPECTOR QUIRK. Oh! on the contrary, the rooms bore every mark of having been recently and hurriedly ransacked.

QUESTIONER. How do you mean?

INSPECTOR QUIRK. Well, sir, clothes lay about the floor with their pockets inside out, drawers stood open, and on the hearth there was pile of ashes, as though important papers had been burned.

QUESTIONER. A pile of ashes, eh? Were you able to find anything there that would give us more knowledge of Hyde and his connection with the crime?

INSPECTOR QUIRK. I'm glad you asked that, sir. To be sure we did. There among the embers was the remains of a green check book.

QUESTIONER. A green check book?

INSPECTOR QUIRK. A green check book.

QUESTIONER. How was that of use?

INSPECTOR QUIRK. How, sir? Well, I'll tell you right away. It had the name of the bank on it, yes sir. And I wasted no time in getting down there to nose it out; and now listen to this, *(proud of his discovery)* I discovered there were several thousand pounds lying in the murderer's account.

QUESTIONER. Then it was a most useful discovery.

INSPECTOR QUIRK. You may depend upon it, sir. "I have him in my hand," I said to myself. "Money's life to a man of his nature. I have nothing to do but wait for him to show up."

QUESTIONER. But he didn't show up, I take it.

INSPECTOR QUIRK. *(deflated)* Well ... no. But in your normal case, with your normal criminal, that would have been the clincher. On the run, without funds, he must come to the bank sooner or later, and then I've got him.

QUESTIONER. But he didn't come, of course.

INSPECTOR QUIRK. No, sir.

QUESTIONER. So that bit of "sleuthing" didn't pay the piper this time.

INSPECTOR QUIRK. *(feeling the put-down)* No, sir.

QUESTIONER. *(changing the questioning)* What have you learned about the background of Mr. Edward Hyde?

INSPECTOR QUIRK. Everything disreputable, sir. Tales of his misdeeds are still coming to light. He was accustomed to mingling with the lowest of the low, I'll tell you that.

QUESTIONER. But aside from his criminal activities, what do you know about the man?

INSPECTOR QUIRK. Nothing. Not a whisper.

QUESTIONER. Nothing? Is there no record of birth?

INSPECTOR QUIRK. None.

QUESTIONER. No family?

INSPECTOR QUIRK. None that we can account for.

QUESTIONER. No professional record?

INSPECTOR QUIRK. No, sir.

ACT TWO 53

QUESTIONER. No ducuments that could shed light on this person's education?

INSPECTOR QUIRK. Not a parcel.

QUESTIONER. No old photographs, newspaper accounts, nothing?

INSPECTOR QUIRK. That is correct, sir, most correct. Except for his unsavory behavior, Mr. Hyde has no past that can be determined. And let me tell you here and now, no future if I could get my hands on him. But I'll say this, it isn't because we haven't made every effort. My work has been thoroughly professional and on the pin head. Mr. Hyde has no past. That's the bull's eye of the matter, sir.

QUESTIONER. So your inspection, sir, has come to naught.

INSPECTOR QUIRK. *(with a victorious chuckle)* Not on your tintype! Begging your honor's pardon, but there is one little item you forgot to ask me about.

QUESTIONER. Ah! you have me there, Inspector. What surprise is in store for us?

INSPECTOR QUIRK. We made a most remarkable discovery at that house in Soho, a piece of evidence that puts the cap on it for Mr. Hyde. The other half of the stick, sir, the murder weapon, was found behind a door.

QUESTIONER. Now, that was a remarkable discovery.

INSPECTOR QUIRK. "I have him in my hand," I said. "The jig's up if we but find him." He must have lost his head or he'd never left the stick. *(pounding decisively on the witness box)* That's hard evidence, sir, hard as nails.

(LIGHTS out on witness box, up on JEKYLL at HIS desk.)

JEKYLL. My exemplary behavior did not last forever. For all my good intentions, I was still cursed with the duality of purpose; and as the first edge of my penitence wore off, the lower side of me, so long indulged, so recently chained down, began to growl for license. Not that I dreamed of resuscitating Hyde, oh no. The bare idea of that would strike me to frenzy. No, it was in my own person that I was once more tempted to trifle with my conscience; and it was as an ordinary secret sinner that I at last fell before the assaults of temptation. Then can it be, I thought, that it is Jekyll, not Hyde, on whom the full measure of guilt can be placed?

(LIGHTS out on JEKYLL, up on MORDANT in the witness box.)

QUESTIONER. How long have you been in the employ of Mr. Hyde?

MRS. MORDANT. *(not eager to cooperate)* Only a year.

QUESTIONER. How were you engaged? Did you answer an advertisement?

MRS. MORDANT. I did not.

QUESTIONER. Then how was Mr. Hyde in touch with you?

MRS. MORDANT. He wasn't.

QUESTIONER. I beg your pardon?

MRS. MORDANT. Mr. Hyde did not engage me.

QUESTIONER. *(a little impatient)* Well, would you please be helpful and explain how you came to be in his employ?

MRS. MORDANT. I was approached by another gentleman. He knew I was in hard times and needed work, bless him.

QUESTIONER. I see. And who was this gentleman?

MRS. MORDANT. *(not answering)* Humph!

QUESTIONER. Mrs. Mordant, you must answer the question.

MRS. MORDANT. *(more emphatically)* Hah!

QUESTIONER. Mrs. Mordant, you are obligated to answer my inquiries. There are penalties for not cooperating.

MRS. MORDANT. *(after a pause)* I don't remember his name.

QUESTIONER. I believe you do. *(impatiently)* See

ACT TWO

here, his name will come out sooner or later, so you had better answer and save yourself a good deal of trouble.

(MORDANT still hesitates.)

QUESTIONER. Let me ask the question again: who was the gentleman that hired you?
MRS. MORDANT. *(pausing again)* His name is Jekyll.
QUESTIONER. Dr. Henry Jekyll?
MRS. MORDANT. It could be.
QUESTIONER. *(more amiably)* Ah, Jekyll again.
MRS. MORDANT. Or maybe not.
QUESTIONER. *(sharply)* Oh, come now, madame, stop toying with me. Was it Dr. Henry Jekyll or was it not?
MRS. MORDANT. I suppose it was. *(stiffly)* Yes, sir. It was Dr. Jekyll.
QUESTIONER. Thank you. Now, would you tell us please how you came to know Dr. Henry Jekyll?
MRS. MORDANT. That would be a private matter and not your concern.
QUESTIONER. Madame, everything is our concern when it is connected with this case. Don't make me caution you again. Now then, how did you come to know Dr. Jekyll?
MRS. MORDANT. *(sullenly)* I ... I have not been well.... To get to the point, I was seriously ill two years ago and Dr. Jekyll attended me. I had no means of payment and he asked for none.
QUESTIONER. Then you are indebted to this man.
MRS. MORDANT. He is a saint among saints. I would do anything for him.
QUESTIONER. I have to agree with you, Mrs. Mordant. Your case is typical of the many charitable acts attributed to Dr. Jekyll. But what of Mr. Hyde, what can you tell us about him?
MRS. MORDANT. I can tell you nothing.
QUESTIONER. You mean you won't.
MRS. MORDANT. I mean what I said. I know nothing

of the man. I rarely saw him, much less talked to him. And I don't go snooping about, if that's what you're getting at.

QUESTIONER. *(chuckling)* Well, I must admit, Mrs. Mordant, that is what I was getting at.

(LIGHTS out on witness box, up on JEKYLL at his desk.)

JEKYLL. Although when I again, as Henry Jekyll, submitted to the urges of my baser side, I was ill at ease, conscious of danger that had long since passed from my mind as Edward Hyde. But soon the old recklessness returned and I was able to enjoy my wanton pursuits freely and without fear of discovery. Yet there comes an end to all things; and this brief condescension to my evil finally destroyed the balance of my soul.

(SOUND of punctuation. LIGHTS dim down on JEKYLL as he continues writing, up on witness box.)

QUESTIONER. Mr. Utterson, can you determine how Mr. Hyde was able to come into such furnishings in what otherwise was a humble house in Soho?

UTTERSON. I can only speculate that since Hyde is a ward of Dr. Jekyll's, the things may have been selected by him. The pictures on the walls were of extraordinary good taste, and Jekyll is much of a connoiseur in that department.

QUESTIONER. This Dr. Jekyll seems to be a man of extraordinary means and ability.

UTTERSON. I certainly can vouch for that, sir.

QUESTIONER. Now, Mr. Utterson, at this time we want to examine the incident of the evening of October 11.

UTTERSON. The eleventh ... yes, that would be ...

QUESTIONER. The day following the murder.

UTTERSON. Yes. ... Well, I had received a note from Jekyll that morning, stating that he wished to see me. As you know, the better part of my day was spent with Inspector Quirk at the house in Soho. Consequently, I went round to

ACT TWO   57

his lodgings as soon as I was able to refresh myself and dress.

QUESTIONER. That would be in the evening of the eleventh?

UTTERSON. Yes.

QUESTIONER. Go on.

UTTERSON. I was admitted by Poole and ushered across the yard to the building which is known as the laboratory or dissecting rooms. I was quite surprised, you see, for it was the first time I had been invited to that part of the house.

QUESTIONER. I see. And what did you find there?

UTTERSON. I must say I have always been most curious about the place, but it wasn't what I had expected.

QUESTIONER. In what way?

UTTERSON. Well, there was no appearance of medical activity, no professional air about the room.

QUESTIONER. Really?

UTTERSON. Rather, it was dingy and windowless; the tables were laden with chemical apparatus and the floor was littered with crates and packing straw.

QUESTIONER. Yes, I can understand your surprise. Continue.

UTTERSON. At the farther end of the place was a flight of stairs which led to rooms used by Jekyll for God-knows-what, some sort of get-away, I suppose. This is where I was taken.

(LIGHTS out on witness box, up on JEKYLL, still seated at HIS desk, looking sickly. POOLE has entered.)

POOLE. Mr. Utterson, sir.
JEKYLL: Oh, yes.

(UTTERSON crosses in. POOLE leaves.)

UTTERSON. Good evening, Harry. Well, look at you. What's the matter? You look like the worst of your patients. Have you been ill?

(JEKYLL shakes hands with UTTERSON without rising.)

JEKYLL. Oh, nothing to worry about, just a touch of something, perhaps some ill-gotten food. Please sit down.

UTTERSON. *(ignoring the invitation)* Well now, have you heard the news?

JEKYLL. They were crying it in the square, "M.P. Brutally Murdered!" I heard them clear in my dining-room.

UTTERSON. Then one word: Carew was my client, but so are you; and I want to know what I'm about in this matter. You've not been mad enough to hide this fellow?

JEKYLL. John, I swear to God I will never set eyes on him again. I bind my honor to you that I am done with him. And indeed he does not want my help; he is safe, quite safe, mark my words. He will never more be heard of.

UTTERSON. You seem to be pretty sure of him; and for your sake, I hope you are right. If it comes to a trial, your name will appear.

JEKYLL. I am quite sure of him. You see, I have grounds for certainty that I can't share with anyone. But rest easy, my friend. *(changing his approach)* Now, there is one thing on which you may advise me. It is the reason I ask for you to come. I have ... uh ... I have received a letter and I am at a loss whether I should show it to the police. I should like to leave it in your hands, John; you will judge wisely, I'm sure.

UTTERSON. Is it that you fear it might lead to Hyde's detection?

JEKYLL. No, I can't say that I care what becomes of Hyde. As I said, I am quite done with him. I was thinking of my own character, which this hateful business has rather exposed.

UTTERSON. *(thinking a moment)* Well, let me see the letter.

(JEKYLL hands HIM the letter without rising, which UTTERSON quickly reads aloud.)

ACT TWO

UTTERSON. "To my benefactor, Henry Jekyll: My dear friend, whom I have so long unworthily repaid for a thousand generosities--" Well, that's the truth. "--you need labor under no alarm for my safety. I have means of escape upon which I place great confidence. Although we will never meet again, I remain your devoted servant, Edward Hyde." Is this signature authentic?

JEKYLL. There is no doubt about it.

UTTERSON. Have you the envelope?

JEKYLL. *(taken by surprise)* What?

UTTERSON. The envelope in which this letter came.

JEKYLL. *(grabbing at a reply)* Oh ... I ... I burned it ... *(seeing UTTERSON'S reaction)* before I thought what I was about. But it bore no postmark. The note was delivered by hand.

UTTERSON. I see. *(thinking a moment)* I shall keep this and sleep on it.

JEKYLL. I wish you to judge for me entirely. I have lost confidence in myself.

UTTERSON. Well, I shall consider.

JEKYLL. *(calling off)* Poole!

UTTERSON. And one word more: was it Hyde who dictated the last terms of your will?

(JEKYLL nods weakly.)

UTTERSON. I knew it! He meant to murder you. You have had a fortunate escape.

JEKYLL. I have had what is far more to the purpose: I have had a lesson; oh, God, John, what a lesson I've had!

(POOLE enters as JEKYLL rises from HIS chair.)

JEKYLL. Show Mr. Utterson out, Poole. *(hurriedly shaking hands with UTTERSON)* Goodbye, John. I look to you to see to my best interests. And now I must go in and rest.

(JEKYLL exits hurriedly. POOLE begins to usher UTTERSON out, but is stopped by UTTERSON'S question.)

UTTERSON. By the bye, there was a letter handed in today. What was the messenger like?
POOLE. You must be mistaken, sir. Nothing has come today except by post, and only circulars at that.

(LIGHTS up on witness box, out on scene. UTTERSON crosses to it.)

QUESTIONER. Well, well! Hyde's letter poses an important question. What do you make of it?
UTTERSON. Well, at the time, I asked myself that if the letter didn't come by messenger as Jekyll claimed, how did it get there? Was it written on the property? And if that were so, it must be differently judged and handled with more caution.
QUESTIONER. Exactly.
UTTERSON. Quite frankly, I was in the midst of a dilemma. My one friend and client had been brutally murdered. Another friend and client was in danger of being sucked down in the eddy of the scandal. It was a ticklish decision I had to make.
QUESTIONER. What did you do?
UTTERSON. I sought advice.
QUESTIONER. From whom?
UTTERSON. From my head clerk, Mr. Guest. I have often confided in him on matters of importance.
QUESTIONER. Then you showed him the document?
UTTERSON. I did. "It's an ugly business at the best," I said, "but there it is, a murderer's autograph."
QUESTIONER. And what was his conclusion?
UTTERSON. He studied it with a passion, looking at it again and again under a glass. Then he went to the cabinet and pulled out one of Jekyll's letters.

ACT TWO

QUESTIONER. Did that strike you as strange?
UTTERSON. Not really. You see, he has been privy to my correspondence with Dr. Jekyll over the years and is familiar with his hand.
QUESTIONER. He compared the signatures?
UTTERSON. He did. And he found a rather singular resemblance. The two were in many points identical, only differently sloped.
QUESTIONER. Then, Mr. Utterson, in your opinion ... ?
UTTERSON. *(with great hesitancy)* Henry Jekyll had forged the signature.

(SOUND emphasis, then subduing and following quietly under dialogue, as LIGHTS go out on the witness box, up on JEKYLL.)

JEKYLL. It was a fine, clear day in December of this same year, wet under foot where the frost had melted, but cloudless overhead. Regent's Park was full of winter as I sat in the sun on a bench, the animal within me licking the chops of memory, the spiritual side a little drowsed, promising subsequent penitence but not yet moved to begin. After all, I reflected, I was like my neighbors. And then I smiled, comparing myself with other men, comparing my active goodwill with the lazy cruelty of other men's neglect. And at the very moment of that vain-glorious thought, a qualm came over me, a horrid nausea and the most deadly shuddering. These passed away and left me faint; and then as in its turn, the faintness subsided. I began to be aware of a change in the temper of my thoughts, a greater boldness, a contempt of danger, a dissolution of the bonds of obligation. I looked down to find my clothes hanging formless on my shrunken limbs; the hand that lay on my knee was corded and hairy. I was once more Edward Hyde.

(SOUND up dramatically. LIGHTS out on JEKYLL, up on witness box.)

QUESTIONER. So, Mr. Utterson, you considered the letter to be counterfeit.

UTTERSON. I did.

QUESTIONER. And what did you do about it?

UTTERSON. Nothing.

QUESTIONER. Nothing?

UTTERSON. Well, Jekyll had committed no crime in writing it; he had merely given it to me. And as his solicitor I felt it prudent to let the letter rest in my files.

QUESTIONER. I see.

UTTERSON. Mind you, I was not pleased with the thought of it, this shallow attempt at protecting his friend Hyde; and, I must say, it weighed on my mind, but ...

QUESTIONER. Alright then, let us move forward. When was the next time you saw Jekyll?

UTTERSON. Let me see ... it was ... on the eighth of December.

QUESTIONER. The eighth? That's some two months following the letter incident. Is that correct?

UTTERSON. Yes. Quite unexpectedly I received an invitation to a small dinner party Jekyll had arranged. It came as a complete surprise.

QUESTIONER. Why a surprise?

UTTERSON. Well, Jekyll had been reclusive and in seeming ill health since October.

QUESTIONER. But now things had changed for the better?

UTTERSON. Oh, yes. I found him in the best of spirits. Lanyon was there and the host looked fondly from one to the other of us as in the old days when we were inseparable friends.

QUESTIONER. Well, it would seem, all was back to normal.

UTTERSON. One would think as much. But then, on the twelfth--only four days later--Jekyll's door was closed to me.

ACT TWO   63

(LIGHTS up on POOLE in doorway.)

POOLE. The doctor is confined to the house and will see no one.
UTTERSON. On the fifteenth I tried again.
POOLE. I'm sorry, sir; the doctor is receiving no callers.

(LIGHTS out on POOLE.)

UTTERSON. Jekyll's reclusiveness began to weigh upon my spirits.
QUESTIONER. But you didn't drop the matter?
UTTERSON. No, sir, I did not.
QUESTIONER. And so ... ?
UTTERSON. So I went round to see Lanyon; I knew, at least, I would be admitted there.
QUESTIONER. And what was the outcome of your visit?
UTTERSON. I was startled. Yes, I was shocked at the change in Lanyon's appearance since I saw him just the few days earlier at Jekyll's dinner party.
QUESTIONER. In what manner had he changed?
UTTERSON. He was pale and visibly thinner; his features resembled a man twenty years his senior.
QUESTIONER. Within only a matter of days, Dr. Lanyon had exhibited such physical decay?
UTTERSON. Yes, it was unbelievable. There was a look in the eye and a quality of manner that seemed to testify to some deep-seated terror of the mind.
QUESTIONER. Terror, you say?
UTTERSON. Yes. It was unlikely that he should fear death, yet that was what I was tempted to suspect.
QUESTIONER. How do you mean?
UTTERSON. He had the warrent of death written legibly upon his face. I couldn't help but remark about the change in his appearance.

(LIGHTS up on LANYON, out on WITNESS BOX. LANYON

has visibly aged. UTTERSON moves into the scene.)

LANYON. Yes, John, I am aware of the way I look. The fact is, I have had a shock from which I will never recover. I'm afraid it is only a question of weeks with me before I am confined to my bed and ... then, who knows?

UTTERSON. But, my dear friend, this is most surprising. What's happened? What is the ...

LANYON. No! Please! Don't ask questions, John, for I am not at liberty to give you answers.

UTTERSON. *(accommodating the request)* Jekyll is ill, too. Have you seen him?

LANYON. *(in an unsteady voice)* I wish to see or hear no more of Harry Jekyll. I am quite done with that person; and I beg you to make no reference to one whom I regard as already dead.

UTTERSON. *(seating himself)* Oh, come now. We are three very old friends. Isn't there anything I can do.

LANYON. No! Nothing can be done. Ask Jekyll if you don't believe me.

UTTERSON. But he won't see me.

LANYON. I am not surprised at that. *(struggling to keep HIMSELF in control)* Someday, John, after I am gone, you may perhaps come to learn the right and wrong of this. And in the meantime, if you can sit and talk to me of other things, it will be most comforting; but if you cannot keep clear of this matter of Jekyll, then go, for I cannot bear it.

UTTERSON. My dear sir, allow me to help.

LANYON. No, John. Words are quite useless. The damage has been done.

(LIGHTS out on scene, up on JEKYLL.)

JEKYLL. The moment before my transformation to Edward Hyde I had had the respect of all men. I was wealthy. I was safe. And now I was a known murderer, hunted, houseless, thrall to the gallows. My reason wavered, but it did

ACT TWO

not fail me utterly. I have more than once observed that, in my second character, my faculties seemed sharpened and my spirits more tensely elastic. Thus it came about that, where Jekyll perhaps might have succumbed, Hyde rose to the importance of the moment. Here I was in Regent's Park, daylight and exposed for all to see. My rehabilitating drugs were in my room: how was I to reach them? That was the problem I set myself to solve. I always keep the laboratory door locked. The only key was in Hyde's clothing, also in my room. If I sought to enter by the house, my servants would consign me to the gallows. I saw I must employ another hand, and thought of Lanyon.

(LIGHTS out on JEKYLL, up on witness box and a weakened and sickly LANYON. The urgency of the moment energizes HIS responses, although at times HE speaks with great effort.)

QUESTIONER. Dr. Lanyon, I regret that circumstances have forced us to bring you here in your condition. And I am sure I need not remind you that you appear before us under oath.
LANYON. I understand.
QUESTIONER. Then will you begin by relating the events of December 9.
LANYON. Yes. On the ninth of December I received by the evening delivery this registered envelope addressed in the hand of my colleague and old school companion, Henry Jekyll.

(LANYON takes the letter from his pocket as LIGHTS come up on JEKYLL.)

JEKYLL. I arranged my clothes as best I could, summoned a passing hansom, and drove to a disreputable hotel in Portland Street that Hyde had made use of in his sport. This was the headquarters from which I composed and sent my letters to Lanyon and Poole.

(LIGHTS out on JEKYLL.)

LANYON. I must say I was surprised by this letter because we were by no means in the habit of correspondence. I had seen the man, dined with him, indeed, the night before. And I could imagine nothing in our intercourse that should justify this letter.

QUESTIONER. And what was the contents of the message?

(LIGHTS up on HYDE at the table down right, reading the letter to HIMSELF.)

HYDE. "You are one of my oldest friends and, although we have differed at times on scientific questions, I cannot remember, at least on my side, any break in our affection. There was never a day when, if you had said to me, 'Jekyll, my life, my honor, my reason, depend upon you,' I would not have sacrificed my left hand to help you...." *(with a gleeful chuckle)*

(LANYON picks up reading the letter aloud.)

LANYON. "... Lanyon, my life, my honor, my reason are all at your mercy. If you fail me tonight, I am lost." *(showing signs of faintness)*

QUESTIONER. Yes, I know this is a great physical strain on you, sir, but get to the point, if you would, please.

LANYON. He asked me to go on an errand to his residence--his man Poole was expecting me.

HYDE. *(continuing reading)* "The door to my room is to be forced. You are to go in alone. Go to the cabinet in the southwest corner, breaking the lock if it be shut, and draw out

ACT TWO

all the contents. This drawer I beg of you to carry back to Cavendish Square exactly as it stands."

LANYON. He was very insistent that all this be completed by the hour of midnight.

QUESTIONER. The thing sounds like a second-rate melodrama at the Adelphi.

LANYON. He expected that the servants would be in bed at that hour and that I would be absolutely alone; at which time I was to admit a man who would present himself in his name, and into whose hands I was to place the drawer I had retrieved from the laboratory room.

HYDE. *(continuing)* "Five minutes afterwards, if you insist upon an explanation, you will learn that these arrangements are of capital importance, and that by the neglect of one of them you might have charged your conscience with my death."

(Lights out on HYDE.)

QUESTIONER. Strange, very strange. What did you do?

LANYON. Well, upon reading the letter, I felt certain my friend was insane; but I also felt duty bound to do as he requested. An appeal so worded could not be set aside without a grave responsibility. So I left the house, got into a hansom, and drove straight to Jekyll's place.

(LIGHTS up on POOLE, out on witness box. LANYON crosses into the scene.)

POOLE: Come in, sir.
LANYON. I have just received a letter from Jekyll.
POOLE. Yes. I have been expecting you.
LANYON. See here, Poole, tell me what this is all about.
POOLE. I am to admit you into the study.
LANYON. *(impatiently)* Yes, yes, I know that, but what's the meaning of it?
POOLE. That is all I know, Dr. Lanyon.

LANYON. There is something strange about this, Poole.
POOLE. I agree, sir.
LANYON. But surely, you must know....
POOLE. No, sir. I have not been imformed beyond what was contained in the letter.
LANYON. Damnit, Poole, this is most untoward, upon my soul it is.
POOLE: Yes, sir. These are strange times, sir, most strange. Please follow me.

(POOLE exits. LIGHTS out on scene, up on witness box as LANYON returns.)

QUESTIONER. Well, well. Poole was as much in the dark about this matter as you were. So then what happened?
LANYON. We immediately went to Jekyll's private rooms, adjacent to his laboratory, and entered by breaking open the door. The cabinet was unlocked. I took out the drawer as instructed and returned to Cavendish Square.
QUESTIONER. You have *piqued* my curiosity, Dr. Lanyon. Tell me quickly: what was the contents of the drawer?
LANYON. There was a package of what seemed to be a simple crystalline salt of a white color and a vial about half full of a red-blood liquor, which was highly pungent to the sense of smell and seemed to me to contain phosphorus and some volatile ether. *(pausing briefly to gain strength)* Of the other ingredients I can make no guess. And there was a book, an ordinary version book, which contained little but a series of dates.
QUESTIONER. The whole affair seems most questionable.
LANYON. That's what I thought. How could these items effect the life of my colleague? Why send a messenger? Why could he not go himself for them? Why all the secrecy? The more I reflected the more I was convinced that I was dealing with a case of cerebral decease.

ACT TWO

QUESTIONER. Having done this chore, you then waited for the arrival of Jekyll's representative?

LANYON. Yes. I sent my servants to bed and then loaded an old revolver, that I might be found in some posture of self-defense.

(There is a SOUND of urgent pounding. LIGHTS up on HYDE.)

LANYON. Well, the clock had scarce struck twelve when there was a knock at the front door.

HYDE. *(moving in)* Good evening, Dr. Lanyon.

LANYON. I asked him if he had come for Dr. Jekyll.

HYDE. *(with a backward glance to check if there was anyone in the street)* Yes, sir. Now then, the drawer, do you have it?

LANYON. I ushered him into my consulting room, keeping one hand on my weapon.

HYDE. *(frantically)* Have you got it? Where is it? Give it me.

(LIGHTS out on witness box. LANYON crosses into the scene, HIS physical well-being as it was earlier in the play.)

LANYON. Come, sir, you forget that I have not yet the pleasure of your acquaintance.

HYDE. What's that?

LANYON. Your identity, sir.

HYDE. *(flying into a rage)* The drawer, give it me.

LANYON. Not a bit of it. Not until I know your credentials. Who are you? What is your name?

HYDE. Hyde is my name.

LANYON. Hyde!

HYDE. Yes, Hyde. *(with mocking anger)* Hyde, Hyde, the cat's outside. *(laughing wildly)*

LANYON. Where is Jekyll? What is the meaning of all this?

HYDE. *(turning to immediate anger)* I have no time to waste on talk. The drawer, Lanyon, give it me.
LANYON. No! I will not. Not until you tell me ...

(HYDE lunges at LANYON and clutches at HIS throat. In the struggle, LANYON pulls HIS gun from beneath HIS coat and fires into the air. HYDE staggers back in surprise.)

LANYON. Control yourself, man, or I shall summon help.
HYDE. *(with false politeness)* I beg your pardon, Dr. Lanyon. What you say is very well founded, and my impatience has shown its heels to my politeness. I come here at the instance of your colleague, Dr. Henry Jekyll, on a piece of business of some moment; and I understood ...*(HIS hand on HIS throat, wrestling with hysteria)* I understood, a drawer ...
LANYON. There it is. *(pointing to the table)* Now kindly explain what this is all about.

(HYDE picks up the drawer and hurries to leave, but is cut off from the door by LANYON.)

HYDE. Out of my way.
LANYON. Not until I get an answer. Where is Jekyll? What is this drawer about?
HYDE. Don't be a fool, man! This is not your concern. I beg you. Allow me to take this drawer and go from your house without further explanation? *(growing convulsive)*
LANYON. Sir, I have been carried too far into this to pause before I see the end.
HYDE. Well then! you have won the spin. *(moving back into the room)* I see I have no choice. But, Lanyon, remember your vows: what follows here is under the seal of your profession. I bind you to your word.

(HYDE, with teeth grating from a convulsive action of HIS

ACT TWO   71

jaws, and a face of ghastly hue, rushes to the table, uttering a piercing sob of relief, and mixes the concoction.)

    LANYON. Compose yourself, man. What are you doing?
    HYDE. *(turning to HIM abruptly)* Had you allowed me to leave, you would be as you were before, none the wiser. But perhaps this is for the best; for now you shall observe and obtain a new form of knowledge, the sight of which could stagger the unbelief of Satan. And now, to settle what remains.

(HYDE raises HIS glass as if for a toast.)

    LANYON. What do you mean?

(HYDE puts the glass to HIS lips and drinks.)

    HYDE. *(with arrogance)* You! You! who have so long been tied to the most narrow and material views, you who have denied the virtue of trans-cendental medicine, you who have derided your superiors--behold!

(Then HYDE utters a loud cry, reels, staggers, falls to the floor and rolls in convulsions. There is an explosion of SOUND as HYDE gradually transforms into JEKYLL. After a moment of calm, HE sits up, revealing himself to LANYON.)

    LANYON. Oh, God! Jekyll!

(LANYON grabs at HIS chest, gasps, sinks to HIS knees, then slowly to the floor. LIGHTS go out on scene accompanied by a thunderous SOUND. As the LIGHTS come up again, the court room has disappeared. JEKYLL is standing down center. The QUESTIONER. is directly behind him, a back light falling over his shoulders.)

QUESTIONER. Well, Harry, this is quite a story, I must say, this amazing transformation in Lanyon's consulting room.

JEKYLL. The shock was too much for him, which is quite understandable.

QUESTIONER. He went into a seizure?

JEKYLL. Yes.

QUESTIONER. And then?

JEKYLL. I checked his pulse. On finding he was alive, I rang for the servants and left without explanation.

QUESTIONER. A cowardly act, leaving a man in such condition and you a doctor.

JEKYLL. I don't deny it. But you must understand what I had gone through all that day and night, what terror I had felt.

QUESTIONER. Alright, then what happened?

JEKYLL. It was partly in a dream that I returned to my home and got into bed.

QUESTIONER. In bed? You went to bed?

JEKYLL. To comfort myself with the assurance of being close to my drugs.

QUESTIONER. And to conceal yourself from shame.

JEKYLL. It's true. And, for a time at least, secure from the arm of the law?

QUESTIONER. Go on.

JEKYLL. When I was once more myself, a change came over me. It was no longer the fear of the gallows, it was the horror of being Hyde that racked me. From that day forth, it seemed only under great effort, and only under the immediate stimulation of the drug, that I was able to wear the countenance of Jekyll. At all hours of the day and night, I would feel the change occurring. Above all, if I slept, or even dozed for a moment in my chair, it was always as Hyde that I awakened. *(fighting to contain HIS emotions)* Under the strain of it all, and by the sleeplessness to which I now condemned myself, I became eaten up by fever, weak in body and mind, and solely occupied by one thought: the horror of my other self. *(breaking into tears and sinking to his knees)*

ACT TWO

QUESTIONER. Brace up, Harry, we must see this through. This other nature of yours, this Edward Hyde, was becoming obsessively stronger.

JEKYLL. *(quietly)* Yes, ... yes, the powers of Hyde seemed to have grown with the sickness of Jekyll. And certainly the hate that now divided us was equal on each side.

QUESTIONER. Can you describe these feelings toward this other self?

JEKYLL. This hatred? Yes. It is a shocking thing, that that which is dead and has no shape is knit to me closer than an eye--here in my flesh, where I hear it mutter and feel it struggle to be born, and I have no power to rid myself of it.

QUESTIONER. And Hyde, what of him?

JEKYLL. The hatred of Hyde for Jekyll is of a different order. His terror of the gallows drives him continually to fits of panic.

QUESTIONER. Yes.

JEKYLL. He resents my hatred of him, hence the ape-like tricks he plays on me.

QUESTIONER. Tricks? What sort of tricks?

JEKYLL. Scrawling, in my own hand, blasphemies on the pages of my books; burning my letters; and destroying the portrait of my father. And indeed, had it not been for his fear of death, he would long ago have ruined himself in order to ruin me. But his love of life is excessive. I know how he fears my powers to cut him off by suicide.

(JEKYLL rises and sits at his desk.)

JEKYLL. And, oh! the irony of it all.

QUESTIONER. Yes?

JEKYLL. It turns out my experiments have been baseless--more an accident than science.

QUESTIONER. How do you mean?

JEKYLL. My provisions of the salt, which had never been renewed since the date of the first experiment, began to run low.

QUESTIONER. What did you do?

JEKYLL. I sent out for a fresh supply, mixed the draught, and drank it. To my surprise, it had no effect.

QUESTIONER. Indeed?

JEKYLL. I sent out for more, had London ransacked for the correct powder. But it was all in vain.

QUESTIONER. Why "in vain?"

JEKYLL. I am now convinced that my first supply was impure.

QUESTIONER. Impure?

JEKYLL. Yes. It was that unknown impurity which caused an accidental miracle.

QUESTIONER. I see. Not the workings of a scientific mind.

JEKYLL. My God, I was so sure of my genius!

QUESTIONER. *(after a pause)* Well, there it is. I take it then that you accept responsibility for what has happened?

JEKYLL. *(After a moment, the answer is almost a whisper.)* Yes.

QUESTIONER. Speak up!

JEKYLL. My answer is "yes."

QUESTIONER. This whole unspeakable series of events as concerns Edward Hyde?

JEKYLL. Yes.

QUESTIONER. For this you accept full and unequivocal blame?

JEKYLL. I do. I am ready for whatever fate may follow.

QUESTIONER. Well said. Well, that's it then. We are finished here.

(The QUESTIONER starts to leaved but is stopped by JEKYLL.)

JEKYLL. Yet, one thing more. Strange as my circumstances were, the terms of this debate are as old and commonplace as man.

QUESTIONER. How do you mean?

ACT TWO 75

JEKYLL. Am I so different? Clearly, much the same inducements cast the die for any tempting and trembling sinner; and it fell out with me, as it falls with so vast a majority of my fellows, that I chose the better part and was found wanting in the strength to keep to it. As I said before, we are all structured for evil, and that's the sum total of it.

(The QUESTIONER disappears.))

JEKYLL. I am finishing this statement under the influence of the last of the old powders. This, then, is the final time, short of a miracle, that Henry Jekyll can think his own thoughts or see his own face in the glass. Nor must I delay too long to bring my writing to an end. Should the throes of change take me in the act of writing it, Hyde will tear it to pieces; but should this letter come into the hands of for whom it is written, Hyde will die upon the scaffold. Or will I find the courage ... *(picking up the glass of liquid from the desk)* ... to release myself at the last moment? *(slowly replacing the glass on the desk)* Still, whatever happens, this is my true hour of death. Here, then, as I seal up my confession, I bring the life of that unhappy Henry Jekyll to an end.

(JEKYLL places his signature on the letter as the LIGHTS fade out. End of play.)

"... It is a shocking thing, that that which is dead and has no shape is knit to me closer than an eye--here in my flesh ..." (page 73)

www.ingramcontent.com/pod-product-compliance
Lightning Source LLC
LaVergne TN
LVHW011215080426
835508LV00007B/803